SYDNEY

By Peter Porter
and the Editors of Time-Life Books

Photographs by Brian Brake

THE GREAT CITIES · TIME-LIFE BOOKS · AMSTERDAM

The Author: Peter Porter is an Australian of English and Scottish descent. He was born in Brisbane in 1929, where his father's family have lived since the 1860s; his mother grew up in Sydney. After working as a journalist in Brisbane, he came to England in 1951 and has earned his living in London since then as a poet, journalist, reviewer and broadcaster. He has made numerous visits to Sydney, and has spent a period as writer-in-residence at Sydney University. Among his published books of poetry are *The Cost of Seriousness* and *Living in a Calm Country*.

The Photographer: Brian Brake was born in Wellington, New Zealand, in 1927. He has worked on assignments for leading international magazines, and ran a documentary film company in Hong Kong until 1976, when he returned to New Zealand. His work has appeared at the New York Museum of Modern Art, and his exhibition "Tanata—The Maori Vision of Man", has toured America and Europe. He has published several books, including *The Sacred Image* (on Thai Buddhist sculpture) and *The Art of the Pacific*.

TIME-LIFE INTERNATIONAL
EUROPEAN EDITOR: Kit van Tulleken
Design Director: Louis Klein
Photography Director: Pamela Marke
Chief of Research: Vanessa Kramer
Special Projects Editor: Windsor Chorlton
Chief Sub-Editor: Ilse Gray

THE GREAT CITIES
Series Editor: Deborah Thompson
Editorial Staff for *Sydney*
Text Editors: Patricia Bahree, John Cottrell, Jane Havell
Designer: Joyce Mason
Picture Editor: Christine Hinze
Staff Writer: Louise Earwaker
Text Researchers: Elizabeth Loving, Liz Goodman, Toni Huberman
Sub-Editor: Nicoletta Flessati
Design Assistants: Susan Altman, Adrian Saunders
Editorial Assistant: Kathryn Coutu
Proof-Reader: Aquila Kegan

Editorial Production
Chief: Ellen Brush
Traffic Co-ordinator: Helen Whitehorn
Picture Department: Sarah Dawson, Belinda Stewart Cox
Art Department: Julia West
Editorial Department: Ajaib Singh Gill

The captions and the texts accompanying the photographs in this volume were prepared by the editors of Time-Life Books.

Valuable assistance was given in the preparation of this volume by Bob Cameron in Sydney.

Published by Time-Life Books (Nederland) B.V.
Ottho Heldringstraat 5, Amsterdam 1018.

© 1980 Time-Life Books (Nederland) B.V.
All rights reserved. First printing in English.

ISBN 7054 0502 8

Cover: In this foreshortened side-view, six of the 10 curving roof-shells that crown the famed Sydney Opera House are transformed into a sharply defined abstract of light and shade.

First end paper: A pelargonium plant thrusts its brilliant blooms through the cast-iron tracery of a balcony on a late-19th-Century house in a Sydney suburb.

Last end paper: Players at a suburban Sydney cricket club compete on a wicket worn bare by heavy use.

THE SEAFARERS
WORLD WAR II
THE GOOD COOK
THE TIME-LIFE ENCYCLOPAEDIA
OF GARDENING
HUMAN BEHAVIOUR
THE GREAT CITIES
THE ART OF SEWING
THE OLD WEST
THE WORLD'S WILD PLACES
THE EMERGENCE OF MAN
LIFE LIBRARY OF PHOTOGRAPHY
THIS FABULOUS CENTURY
TIME-LIFE LIBRARY OF ART
FOODS OF THE WORLD
GREAT AGES OF MAN
LIFE SCIENCE LIBRARY
LIFE NATURE LIBRARY
YOUNG READERS LIBRARY
LIFE WORLD LIBRARY
THE TIME-LIFE BOOK OF BOATING
TECHNIQUES OF PHOTOGRAPHY
LIFE AT WAR
LIFE GOES TO THE MOVIES
BEST OF LIFE

Contents

I.

Gifts of Climate and the Sea

All of my earliest memories of Sydney centre on the magnificent harbour. And that is just as it should be; any account of Sydney, now the capital of the State of New South Wales and the busiest port in the Southern Hemisphere, should start with that great stretch of water that penetrates to the heart of the city. The harbour helped to determine the site of the city—the first European settlement on the Australian continent—when it was founded in 1788 as a remote British penal colony peopled only by a handful of marines, most without wives or families, and several hundred transported convicts. In the early years of hardship and struggle the harbour received the ships and supplies from Britain on which the settlers depended for their very survival. When the colony at last began to thrive and shed its convict past, the city's prosperity was founded on its function as a great port.

I was brought up in hot, dry Brisbane, 470 miles north; but my mother was originally from Sydney and I spent six weeks there at the height of the summer each year during the 1930s and 1940s, staying with my grandmother on the harbour's north shore in the suburb of Woolwich.

My grandmother's single-storey stone house, with a deep and sombre cellar, stood at the very tip of the Woolwich promontory. Along the winding road that led out to it, each of the houses had pleasant grounds, steeply terraced to accommodate the sharp slope down to the water's edge. I learnt to swim and to sail in the waters of the Lane Cove River, which flows into the harbour between Woolwich and greenly overgrown Greenwich, the neighbouring suburb.

There was always plenty of traffic on the river. Ferries passed to and fro on the routes connecting different points on the huge harbour's intricately indented coastline. The brassy Show Boat—used for pleasure cruises and dances—was always announced by its blaring music and the periscope-like progress of its tall smoke-stack, visible long before it came into view around a bend in the river. There were yachts of all sizes, from gin-palace motor cruisers and ocean-going racing craft to the simplest dinghy with a single sail. And the prawn-fishing boats—each rowed by a man standing up, like a Venetian gondolier—were beautiful to see at night across the water, with a soft effulgence around their gunwales from the lanterns that hung at their sterns.

Sydney must be one of the most topographically convoluted cities in the entire world; and the harbour—dividing and yet linking the city's different parts into a whole—is the key to unravelling its complexities. The coastline of the Australian continent's south-eastern seaboard,

Sydney's Opera House (foreground), which opened in 1973 to worldwide acclaim for its breathtaking design, dominates Bennelong Point and the waterfront of Sydney's central business district at Circular Quay. Beyond, to the south, sprawl the suburbs of the city, Australia's largest. Originally known as Sydney Cove, this area—one of many inlets on the southern shore of Sydney's enormous harbour—became the site of the continent's first European settlement founded in 1788.

A deeply sun-tanned young woman on a suburban street matches fashion to the dictates of Sydney's long, warm summers and its dedication to a relaxed lifestyle. The city's temperatures average a benign 72°F for seven months of the year and the winters are so mild that houses must be heated only rarely.

where Sydney is situated, is full of inlets, jutting headlands and river estuaries—a flooded coastline, formed in the remote past when, with the partial melting of the Antarctic ice-cap as the Ice Ages ended, the sea-level rose enough to penetrate into the nooks and crannies of valleys and surface undulations. The great harbour of Sydney, through which the Parramatta River and the smaller Lane Cove River drain eastwards into the Pacific Ocean, was formed by this process of flooding. At the harbour's eastern end, the tides of the Pacific Ocean enter between the North and South Heads—the promontories at the edge of the open sea that guard the mouth like gateposts.

Altogether, the harbour—21 square miles of sheltered water and 152 miles of foreshore—encompasses literally hundreds of bays, inlets, creek mouths, moorings, basins, enclosed dock areas, islands and beaches. It is made up of three chief bodies of water: the main, deep-water harbour is named Port Jackson; at its mouth lies Middle Harbour, a stretch of water between the bluff of North Head and the long tongue of South Head; and all those shallower reaches of water to the west of Port Jackson are reckoned to be part of the Parramatta River. The focus of city and harbour alike is Sydney Cove, a pocket on the south shore of Port Jackson, where the original settlers landed to begin their life on a totally unfamiliar continent 12,000 miles from home.

In my youth, Sydney seemed to be, above all, a city of ferries. In fact, the opening in 1932 of the Sydney Harbour Bridge, linking the north and south shores by road, had already reduced the importance of the ferries from their earlier heyday, but to me they were always the most obvious sights on the blue arms of the harbour, whichever way you looked. For many years my mental map of the city remained organized according to the ferry routes that joined the suburbs around the harbour shores with each other and with Sydney Cove; and my early view of Sydney's character was similarly matched to the leisurely tempo of that most idyllic form of public transport. Many a Sydney story and poem has been composed on the longer ferry trips, which can take up to three-quarters of an hour, and the constantly changing perspectives on the harbour shore, as seen from the ferries by day and night, make up part of the popular iconography of the city in films, paintings and photographs.

Kings of the fleet in those days were the green, white and black Manly ferries, boasting either one or two business-like funnels. All the ferry routes started from Circular Quay, the main waterfront at Sydney Cove. The place was originally called Semicircular Quay because, when it was completed in 1854, the waterfront curved around all three shores of the cove. Since then the name has been abbreviated and its application extended to encompass the modern high-rise business district that lies immediately inland. There has been nothing circular about the quay itself since the 1950s; development in the years since has created a rectangular basin, within which there are five landing stages sticking out like the prongs of a fork, and a single wharf that can accommodate a modern international cruise ship.

After leaving Circular Quay, the Manly ferries carrying homeward-bound commuters proceeded through the main harbour of Port Jackson, east of the Sydney Harbour Bridge and towards the Pacific Ocean. They passed Middle Head—an inner promontory that projects towards South Head and marks the mouth of Port Jackson—and forged across the Pacific swell entering Middle Harbour. The route terminated at Manly Beach just in the lee of North Head and, being double-ended, the ferries then made the return journey without having to manoeuvre to turn round.

These ships were large vessels, some of which came to Australia under their own steam from shipbuilders in Scotland in the 1920s and 1930s. They were capable of carrying up to 1,500 passengers—grand craft with steel hulls, triple decks and superstructures all adorned with polished brass. Their strange-looking names—such as Curl Curl and Dee Why—were taken from the beaches that run in an orderly sequence of bays and headlands up the Pacific coast beyond North Head.

The route served all those who made their homes in the suburbs spreading along behind those northern beaches. Their journey to and from work in central Sydney would otherwise have been an impossibly long detour around the harbour. Reaching the ferry at Manly by tram or bus, commuters bound for work in the city were able to make the second part of the journey as a pleasant seven-mile harbour cruise, travelling in mid-channel with a superb view of the red roofs and terraced gardens of all the harbourside suburbs. On the way home at night the ferry trip was known to afford a frequently welcome opportunity to sober up in the fresh sea breeze, following after-work drinking sessions spent in the pubs around Circular Quay.

The Manly ferries were the only ones that ventured out of the inner harbour. Those that plied between the main harbourside suburbs within Port Jackson were themselves substantial vessels, but obviously designed for quieter waters than were the Manly ships. The suburbs that had spread eastwards from Sydney Cove along the south shore (collectively known as the eastern suburbs) needed no ferries, since the roads to the centre were short and direct; but the occupants of the thickly populated and prosperous suburbs on the north shore required scheduled ferry services.

The third kind of ferry I recall from those days belonged to the so-called Lady Class—all named after the wives of past governors of New South Wales. Smaller than the other ferries but highly esteemed for their beautiful up-to-date diesel engines (their larger sisters on the eastern routes were still using steam power), they ran mostly on routes above the Sydney Harbour Bridge, westwards into the pockets and inlets of the harbour as it narrows into the waters of the Parramatta and Lane Cove

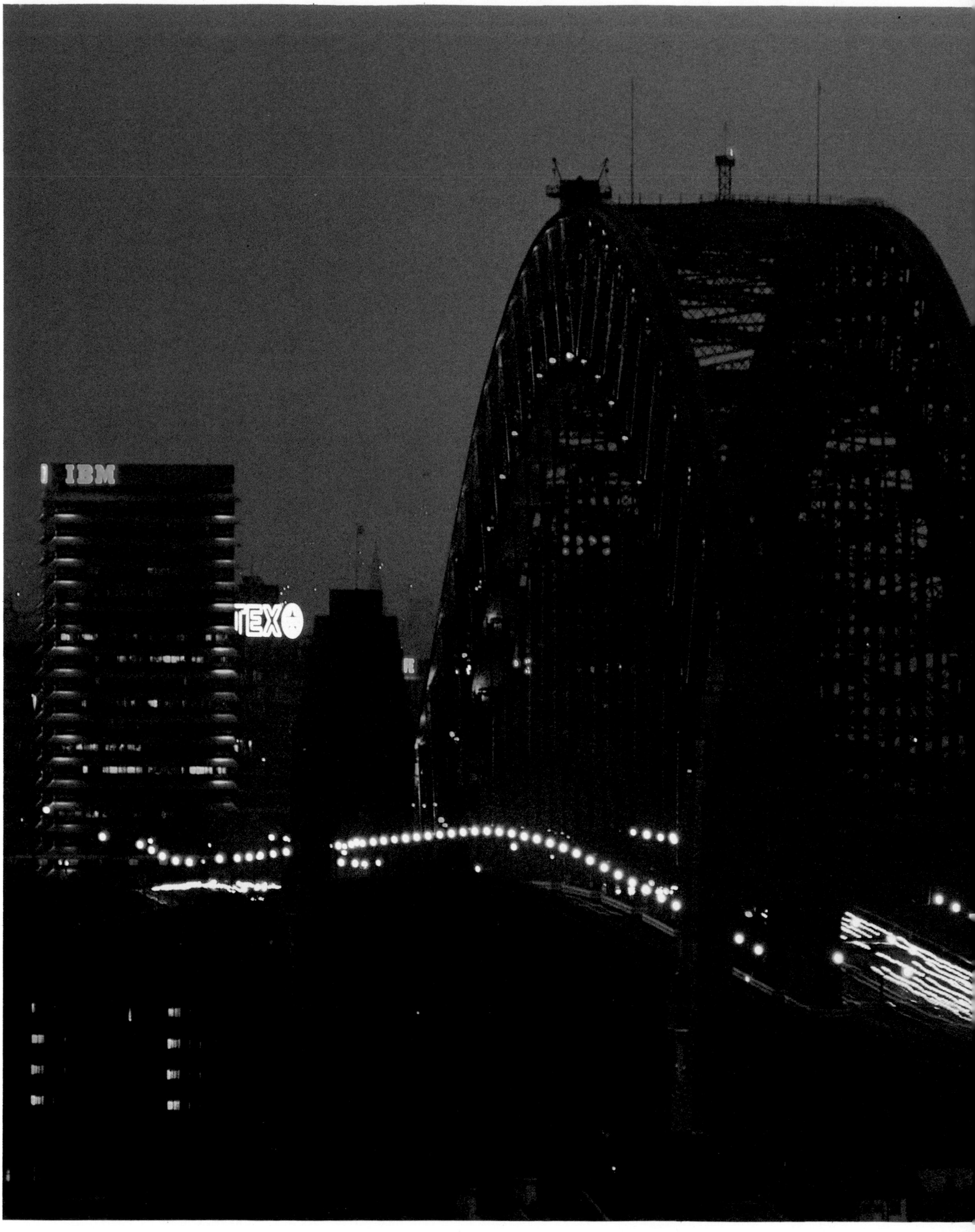
IBM
TEX

Ribbons of light, formed by the beams of nose-to-tail traffic, stretch across Sydney Harbour Bridge as commuters leave the city's business centre for their suburban homes on the north shore. Every work day, more than 140,000 vehicles cross the great arched bridge which was finally completed in 1932.

rivers. I recall with nostalgia evenings at Circular Quay after a day spent in town, waiting for the next ferry back to my grandmother's house at Woolwich, whiling away the time buying the splendid harbour prawns and bottled Hawkesbury oysters, which came from the estuary of the Hawkesbury River just beyond the boundary of Sydney's urban district, 20 miles or so to the north.

I always used to hope the next boat in would be the Lady Chelmsford, if only because she was the oldest of them and had the highest funnel. Due to the many stops, the trip back was not quick; it took about 40 minutes to cover the two and a half miles, but it was always delightful. If you didn't want to look out at the ever-changing waterside panorama, you could wander down to the open engine-room and admire the engineer with his rags and oilcan as he attended the shining engine, all burnished brass and massive flywheels.

The ferry went first to Darling Street Wharf, thence to Goat Island, 440 yards offshore in mid-harbour, then Long Nose Point, Cockatoo Island, Greenwich, and at last Woolwich, where I got off. Then it continued up the Lane Cove River to unknown places that were just names to me: Longueville, Fig Tree, Gladesville. Much later, when I rediscovered Sydney from a different perspective, I once drove in towards the city centre from the north-west, through the Lane Cove National Park, a stretch of country along the river that has been preserved from development. I was startled to realize that those places up the river that I had considered impossibly remote were really part of inner Sydney. Such is the puzzling intricacy of the layout imposed on the city by its harbour setting.

There was a long gap in my acquaintance with Sydney, during which I lived and worked in England; but in 1975, when I was invited to spend a period as writer-in-residence at Sydney University, I had my first glimpse of the city in 20 years. Since then I have been back regularly and now know a new city, full of a palpable sense of awakening.

The Opera House, located at the tip of the tongue of land jutting out on the eastern side of Sydney Cove, and whose distinctive design, since its opening in 1973, has become familiar the world over, seems to hover, like some Valhalla displaced from its misty Nordic heights, in the brilliant southern sunshine. Clusters of high-rise buildings have sprung up in the city centre and even spread to the north shore, making the harbour frontages look like a junior version of the Chicago lakeside skyline; an elevated road and railway situated above Circular Quay feeds traffic on and off the Sydney Harbour Bridge; while almost four miles west, up the harbour, the beautiful, shining-white parabola of the new Gladesville Bridge, built between 1960 and 1964, provides a second link between the north and south shores of the harbour. But amid all the changes, the same essential harmony that I remember remains unimpaired among

blue water, blue skies and the thickly wooded shores that give the harbour its characteristic pleasure-garden appearance.

Inevitably I find myself regretting some of this change. The ferry services available 40 years ago have been curtailed; in the 1950s, in common with every other misguided city, Sydney submitted to a combination of lobbying by the automobile industry and the high cost of labour, and severely reduced its reliance on the ferries. Now many commuters have no choice but to travel by road, and at peak hours traffic piles up disastrously along the highway approaches to both the Gladesville and Sydney Harbour bridges. Today, if you want to travel fast on the Manly route, you take a small, sleek hydrofoil—and see nothing during the journey but the spray whipped up by its jets.

Yet, some traces of the more leisurely era remain: two of the majestic Manly vessels still ply the old route (though they were long ago converted to diesel power) and many occupants of the northern suburbs rely on these old ferries for much of their travelling. For me, one of Sydney's most romantic sights is still provided by a stout and friendly ferry, full of homeward-bound shoppers and children, waddling through the water as it rounds the point on the way to a wharf at, say, Mosman Bay.

Even if most of Sydney's commuters may now prefer to crawl across the bridges in a queue of cars rather than arrive in comfort at the city centre via water, the harbour itself is busier than ever. The volume of cargo shipping is constantly high in this international port; but it is the mixture of commerce and pleasure, side by side, that gives Sydney Harbour its unique flavour. There has been an enormous increase in the number of private craft of all kinds since the days when I was learning to negotiate my small dinghy out of the path of the oncoming Show Boat. All over the

A Sprawl of Harbours and Hinterland

Situated on Australia's south-eastern coast and commanding one of the world's most spectacular deep-water harbours, Sydney has grown in less than two centuries from a tiny penal colony of about a thousand souls into a sprawling conurbation with a population of more than three million. The city is the capital of New South Wales, one of the Australian Commonwealth's seven federated states.

The inset map encompasses the exurban growth that has spread in all directions from the original settlement at Sydney Cove on the harbour's south shore—spilling inland across the coastal plain as far as the Blue Mountains 50 miles away and extending 35 miles along the Pacific coasts from the Ku-ring-gai Chase National Park in the north to the Royal National Park in the south. The city, which covers 4,650 square miles, is Australia's largest urban area.

The large map of the city's central district serves to magnify the complex shape imposed by the harbour's intricate shoreline. Within the North and South Heads that flank the harbour's mouth, the waters of Middle Harbour, Port Jackson and the Parramatta River divide the residential suburbs of the north shore from the five-square-mile business district at Circular Quay and the older, inner-city suburbs that surround it.

The silhouettes mark the locations of some of Sydney's most prominent land-marks and amenities. Others—such as the national parks or the airport and oil refineries of industrialized Botany Bay (inset map)—are in outlying parts of the city. But most—including the Harbour Bridge and the Opera House—are concentrated around the heart of the city at Circular Quay.

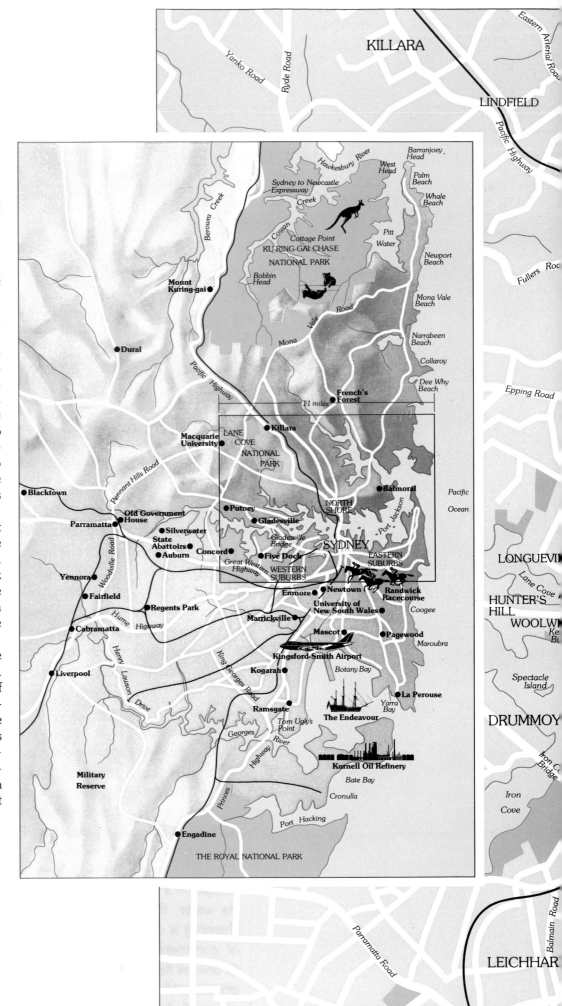

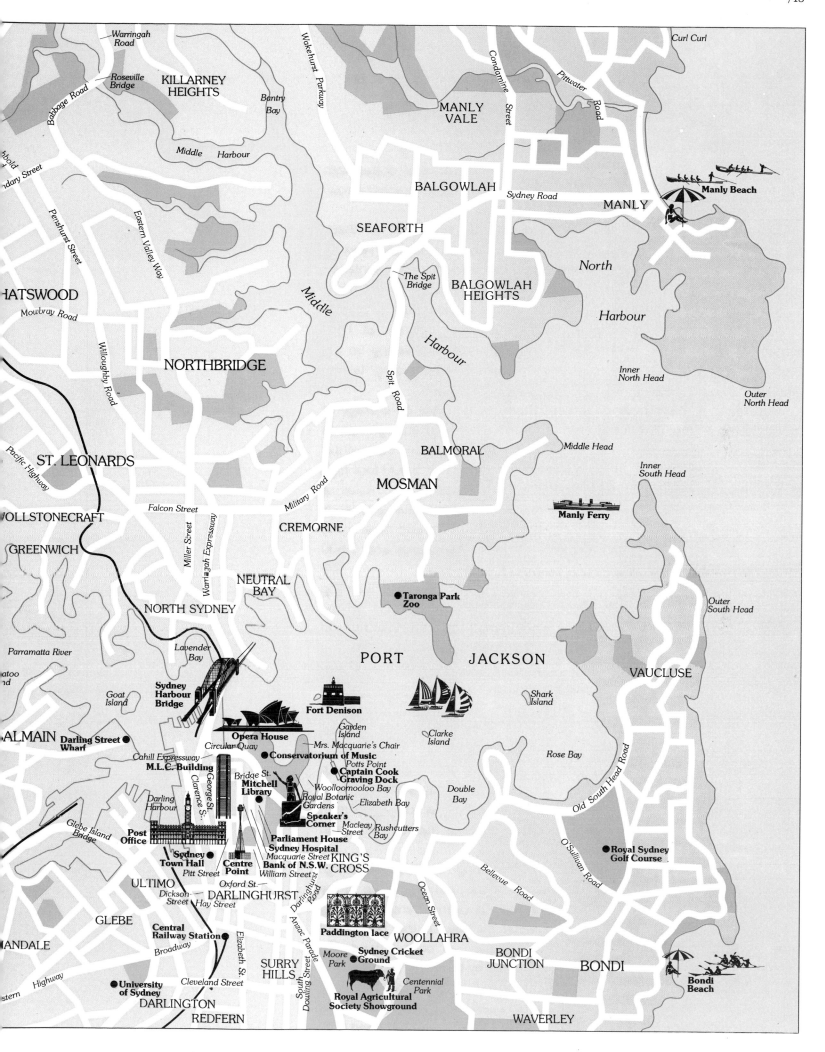

Warringah Road
Roseville Bridge
Babbage Road
KILLARNEY HEIGHTS
Bantry Bay
Wakehurst Parkway
Condamine Street
Pittwater Road
Curl Curl
MANLY VALE
Middle Harbour
BALGOWLAH
Manly Beach
Sydney Road
MANLY
SEAFORTH
HATSWOOD
Mowbray Road
Eastern Valley Way
NORTHBRIDGE
Willoughby Road
Penshurst Street
The Spit Bridge
BALGOWLAH HEIGHTS
North Harbour
Middle Harbour
Spit Road
Inner North Head
Outer North Head
Pacific Highway
ST. LEONARDS
Falcon Street
Military Road
BALMORAL
Middle Head
Inner South Head
WOLLSTONECRAFT
Miller Street
Warringah Expressway
MOSMAN
CREMORNE
Manly Ferry
GREENWICH
NEUTRAL BAY
NORTH SYDNEY
Taronga Park Zoo
Outer South Head
Parramatta River
Lavender Bay
PORT JACKSON
VAUCLUSE
atoo nd
Goat Island
Sydney Harbour Bridge
Shark Island
Fort Denison
ALMAIN
Darling Street Wharf
Opera House
Circular Quay
Garden Island
Clarke Island
Rose Bay
Cahill Expressway
M.L.C. Building
Conservatorium of Music
Potts Point
Captain Cook Graving Dock
Double Bay
Darling Harbour
George St.
Clarence St.
Bridge St.
Mitchell Library
Woolloomooloo Bay
Royal Botanic Gardens
Elizabeth Bay
Glebe Island Bridge
Post Office
Speaker's Corner
Macleay Street
Rushcutters Bay
Royal Sydney Golf Course
Sydney Town Hall
Pitt Street
Centre Point
Parliament House
Sydney Hospital
Macquarie Street
Bank of N.S.W.
William Street
KING'S CROSS
Old South Head Road
O'Sullivan Road
ULTIMO
Oxford St.
Dickson Street
DARLINGHURST
Hay Street
Darlinghurst Road
Anzac Parade
Ocean Street
Bellevue Road
GLEBE
Central Railway Station
Broadway
Elizabeth St.
Paddington lace
WOOLLAHRA
BONDI JUNCTION
BONDI
ANDALE
Cleveland Street
SURRY HILLS
Moore Park
Sydney Cricket Ground
Bondi Beach
stern Highway
University of Sydney
DARLINGTON
REDFERN
South Dowling Street
Royal Agricultural Society Showground
Centennial Park
WAVERLEY
Middle Harbour

harbour you can find one vista after another of calm water dotted with yachts at anchor, children playing about in dinghies, crews practising rowing, others running out their racing craft.

Sydney's incomparable climate is the gift that summons all these pleasure-seekers to the water and gives the city its uniquely relaxed, open-air character. It is as if the Australians ended the long prison sentence that began with their ancestors' release from the weather of northern Europe to discover the sun shining, the waters sparkling and the birds singing; and developed a compulsion to be out there enjoying it all. They certainly do enjoy it—not only lying on the beaches and sailing on the water, but eating out of doors, drinking out of doors, reading, talking and playing out of doors.

Sydney, at a latitude of 33° south of the equator, has an average of seven hours of sunshine a day throughout the year and enough rain (a moderate 47 inches annually, falling mainly in the autumn and early winter between April and June) to keep it from parching. The 3,000-foot-high Blue Mountains, lying roughly parallel with the coast but 50 miles or so inland, divide the narrow coastal plain from the extensive grasslands and the desert—the "dead centre" of the world's driest and most thinly populated continent which stretches 2,000 miles westwards and 1,600 miles north into the tropics.

The blocking mountains cause the damp winds from the Pacific to drop their moisture on the temperate coastal plain, where Sydney lies. At the same time, the harbour escapes the flooding and silting that might result if it received, through the two main rivers that flow into it, all the rain run-off from the Blue Mountains; instead, the Hawkesbury River west of Sydney curves around the city and channels most of the streams descending from the mountains into the sea to the north.

Sydney's average annual temperature is 63°F, and in summer it regularly reaches the high 90s. Indeed, a cynical friend of mine from the relatively cool island of Tasmania, a hundred miles south of Australia's south coast, asserts that in the heat of summer any real thinking is impossible in Australia north of Melbourne (which lies 440 miles further south-west than Sydney); anywhere nearer the equator than that, he maintains, the sun simply fries men's brains in their heads.

I would modify his exaggeration by pointing out that the high temperature (and, still more, the presence of the unmasked sun in the cloudless sky) has produced a special sort of lotus-eating mentality among Sydneysiders. They set as much store by the life of the body—not necessarily strenuous or competitive life either—as of the mind. On beaches around the harbour the style is typified by the hedonists—young, old and middle-aged—who come down to the shore to swim, drink beer, talk and soak up the liberating sun. Even on weekdays, when most people are at work, there seem to be plenty of Sydneysiders at leisure. Retired men

Beer can in hand, a bare-chested umpire signals a wide delivery from the bowler during a cricket match played on waste ground near the popular Rose Bay yachting centre on the south shore of the harbour (background). Cricket—Australia's national summer sport—commands so much enthusiasm that open spaces all over the city are constantly utilized for makeshift games.

and women meet and talk, hats and handkerchiefs over their heads; mothers and children play contentedly; students, fresh from the water, lie reading Dostoevsky, George Eliot, Samuel Beckett, or one of the cult paperbacks on whatever philosophy currently happens to be sweeping the Western student world.

In a city with weather like this, everyone wants to live near the water—and, with so much coastline, many of the wealthier can. A visitor may find himself at an alfresco party in an inner suburb, on the south shore in the older part of the city, one that is hardly renowned for its natural beauty, only to discover when he chases a ball for someone's offspring that the back garden ends suddenly in an old mossy boat-landing that is screened from the house by a thicket of bamboo or an ancient Moreton Bay fig tree—a native species that can grow more than a hundred feet high. As well as a car parked near the house, there may be a 12-foot sailing boat drawn up on the grass, or a waterlogged dinghy tied to a crumbling boatshed. In a different suburban venue—say, the winding, narrow streets of Hunter's Hill, a privileged suburb located on the north shore—he may find, instead of an overgrown garden leading down to the water, a view from a window of a wide sweep of blue sea with its complement of white yachts at anchor.

In the eastern suburbs, where many of Sydney's wealthy professionals live, I find the luxurious conditions rather smooth and characterless, but perhaps I am too easily put off by the sight of thousands of yachts moored side by side. I remember spending one evening in a superb house overlooking Rose Bay, the first of the scalloped curves as you go from South Head along the south coast inside Port Jackson. My host, who was a doctor, indicated to me the descending levels of his estate stretching below us down to the water. At the first level below the house was his swimming pool; then came a terraced garden leading to a street where his large garage was recessed into solid rock; across the road the ground dropped again to the waterside where, at the sea-level itself, his yacht rode conveniently at anchor.

I could certainly appreciate his pleasure as he looked out over the bay, especially since he had arrived in Sydney as a penniless refugee from Europe about 30 years previously. But, even so, I prefer the more intimate and immediate presence of the water that can be found in many other nooks and crannies of the harbour. The recesses of Middle Harbour, for instance, that lead away between wooded green banks north-westwards beyond Middle Head, have something of the aspect of a waterway in a jungle rather than one in the suburbs of a city, except where veranda'd villas and fancifully designed roofs top the skyline.

Harbour views and river views are much in demand but, of course, the most favoured—and expensive—are the ocean views. To work in town and come home at night to the sound of the rollers beating upon the sands in front of your house is an ambition that, in Sydney, is realizable. Down at the beaches south of the Heads—such as Bondi and Bronte—only five miles from central Sydney, huge apartment blocks with façades like Thirties cinemas, or like the bridges of Atlantic liners, flank the esplanades. But up at Narrabeen and Newport, 12 miles or so north along the Pacific coast—suburbs that are both seaside resorts and homes for commuters— old bungalows are still to be found at the edge of the water. Your reprieve from the unnatural world of shops and offices is there before your eyes; and, if you have to work even harder and must mortgage your life for ever to satisfy your lust for the natural beauty of the ocean, the paradox does not seem to embarrass the people who have succeeded in achieving some kind of seaside home.

As Australia's first and oldest city, Sydney has priority both in status and in history. It began as a man-made hell in paradisiacal conditions, where the British dumped the moral casualties of their 18th-Century society—not in an effort to improve their lot but to empty over-crowded prisons and to pre-empt any territorial claims in the South Pacific that might have been made by their contemporary enemies, the French. Even though Sydney is not Australia's political centre, but simply the capital of one of the seven federal states, its historic role as the absolute starting-point of the nation makes it the country's emotional capital.

For 16 years after its founding in 1788, Sydney (together with the nearby colony at Parramatta, where the governor's residence was built) was the

This aerial perspective on Ramsgate, a residential district on Botany Bay, south of central Sydney, offers a representative view of a middle-class Sydney suburb. Some 65 per cent of the city's families are home-owners and many choose to have their own pool, privately supplementing the abundance of swimming facilities available at numerous beaches nearby.

only formal settlement in Australia. (At that time the whole eastern half of the Australian continent was known as New South Wales.) Hobart in Tasmania, settled in 1804, was an offshoot from Sydney. Perth, now the capital of the vast State (nearly a million square miles) of Western Australia, was founded in 1829 by free settlers from Britain. Melbourne, always Sydney's rival for primacy in Australia, came into being in the 1830s and, in 1851, became the capital of the State of Victoria, carved from land that until then had been the southern part of New South Wales. Adelaide, the capital of South Australia, was settled in the 1830s, and Brisbane was made the capital of Queensland (also detached from the old New South Wales) in 1859. Darwin in the far north is the capital of the Northern Territory, an area given self-government in 1978; settled in 1863, its population was still less than 50,000 at the end of the 1970s.

The pattern of settlement in Australia, a country which has always grown by external immigration as well as by internal increases and development, has, since the first colonization, been predominantly urban and coastal. In spite of—or perhaps because of—the continent's immense size of almost three million square miles, and its small population of 14 to 15 million people, about 70 per cent of Australians live in cities and towns, three-quarters of them on the coastal crescent in the south-eastern part of the continent. Australia's five largest mainland cities are all on the coast: ports that became the capitals of independent British colonies. Since Australian federation in 1901 they have been state capitals in a nation modelled on the pattern of the United States. The only inland city with a population that exceeds 200,000 is Canberra, the federal capital that was expressly created, between 1915 and 1927, as a compromise site, thus solving the long-standing rivalry for leadership between Sydney and Melbourne. The small (926-square-mile) Australian Capital Territory, set up to contain the capital 150 miles south-west of Sydney, is inside New South Wales, on rolling plains not far from the Australian Alps.

It is sometimes said of Australians that they all look to Sydney as the authentic embodiment of their country's character. Although Melbourne energetically presses its claims to that status and, in fact, served as the federal capital from 1901 until the function was transferred to Canberra in 1927, it cannot match Sydney's legendary significance. Melbourne has to be content with the title of "the banking capital" and to put up with the reputation of being too imitative of things British. Adelaide is known as "the city of churches" because of its two cathedrals and its numerous places of worship. Perth—2,000 miles away on the far side of the continent and the only Australian city facing the Indian Ocean—is measured as a charming look-out point for the distant world. Brisbane, twined around a snaking river in the "deep north", is an isolated capital whose 19th-Century architecture seems somewhat incongruous in subtropical latitudes. Little Hobart on Tasmania's south shore, with a total population of fewer than 200,000, might still be a penal colony for all the attention that most mainland Australians seem to pay it.

Sydney is not only the oldest city in Australia, it is also the largest. Its outermost suburban boundary encompasses 4,650 square miles. It reaches some 35 miles from its southern limit at the Royal National Park, beyond Botany Bay and Port Hacking, northwards into the Ku-ring-gai Chase National Park. It spreads inland along and beyond the Parramatta River, reaching the Blue Mountains, and its suburbs straggle out into the hinterland so far that it is not easy to judge where the city ends and the bush begins. With fewer than 3.5 million inhabitants by the late 1970s, Sydney can offer its citizens space as well as size.

The suburban style of Australian cities is one of the aspects most often commented on, and in this—as in many things—Sydney is never less than typically Australian. The ideal of home ownership and a garden for every house is deeply entrenched in the ambitions of Australians. Many of them are exiles, or the descendants of exiles, from the cramped cities of Europe, who left behind them—voluntarily or involuntarily—a world in which the power of the landlord and the powerlessness of the tenant had been amply demonstrated. The result, in a country where space is apparently unlimited, has been cities that sprawl for miles, to allow as many people as possible to own a bungalow, with a garden front and back, and preferably a garage as well.

Sydney also has many blocks of apartments (in Australia known as "home units"), especially in the older and more densely populated regions and on sites near the harbour—enough to have earned itself identification as Australia's most Americanized city. But the territorial imperative, always strong in the Sydneysider, has been reinforced by prohibitively high rents, and many high-rise block dwellers actually buy their apartments—taking out property rights on a cube of space in mid-air—instead of renting; the rest of the tenants consider an apartment merely a transitional stage on the route to home ownership.

But, however typical Sydney is in its suburban development, it is also unique. Sydney owes its special interpretation of the normal lifestyle in Australia—as it owes so much else—to its spectacular geography, to which it is, and always will be, a willing captive. In a city that is almost a series of islands, the difficulties of communication and transport tend to keep different districts somewhat separated from each other—an effect also fostered by the huge extent of the built-up area. Consequently many of those suburbs which were once separate towns have preserved their distinctness even under the standardizing influences of the present day. Sydneysiders know that they belong to a great city, but much of their affection and loyalty is reserved for their suburbs.

Poring over a map of Sydney will bring some understanding of the city's physical layout, but for the stranger it will never have the same significance as it does for the Sydney resident. The map shows the places, but not their emotional relationship to each other, or the individual connotations roused by the very names of the different regions.

Some names hark back to the country's early settlers; they were originally given to the small homesteads they set up, later to be swallowed by the expanding city: Lavender Bay, Mosman, Point Piper, French's Forest, Milson's Point, Davidson Park. Since the colonists were Britons with a nostalgia for the land of their birth, they also imported names well-known to them at home: suburbs called Putney, Greenwich and Woolwich recall some of the villages and towns which in those days surrounded London. London's Hyde Park has given its name to a smaller Sydney park, but Regent's Park in Sydney is a suburb. Scottish and Irish names are legion too: Balmoral, Argyle, Sutherland, Bantry Bay, Killarney. All over Sydney, these old and well-loved names, transplanted from the British Isles, jostle with the sounds of words representing the settlers' imitations of the languages spoken by Australia's Aboriginal inhabitants: Narrabeen, Woollahra, Kogarah, Turramurra, Warrawee, Waitara.

From the original settlement at Sydney Cove the city grew—first spreading straight back inland to form the area now known as the central business district, which encompasses about five square miles; then outwards to form concentric rings—or rather semicircles—of suburbs on the harbour's south shore. At the same time, the north shore was gradually colonized, and the city spread westwards by degrees along both banks of the Parramatta River. Suburbs also crept out to line the magnificent, surf-bordered beaches facing the Pacific—first to the south of the Heads near the city centre, then further and further up the north coast. Southwestwards, into the flat, low-lying hinterlands away from the seashores, the city spread for mile after mile; and industrial development gradually surrounded the broad inlet of Botany Bay, six miles down the coast from the harbour mouth.

Sydney's architecture is as various as its scenery; every kind of European tradition seems to have served as a model at one time or another. Australian architecture in general has come in for much criticism and in Sydney there is no shortage of what Melbourne architect Robin Boyd has called "the great Australian ugliness"—sometimes due to the faceless sameness of red-roofed villas, sometimes to the perverse individuality of a house imitating a crofter's cottage or a Swiss-style chalet. But, in Sydney's case, the overall impression left by so many different styles and their local mutations is one of sheer exuberance.

Over many of the harbour's secluded bays and inlets, a large official building presides, usually perched on the highest vantage point, and churches also often enjoy the good fortune of the finest and most dominating sites. Citizens of Hunter's Hill, for instance, on the shores of the Lane Cove River, cannot forget the lordly presence of St. Joseph's College,

For sale on a stall at a street fair in the smart inner suburb of Woollahra, this ingenious construction, fashioned with parts of old clocks and watches, represents the Opera House and the Harbour Bridge—the two landmarks that have become the city's informal emblems.

invincibly far above the beautiful, late-colonial houses of the suburb. At Manly, the great seminary of St. Patrick's College overlooks the garish seaside front with its pubs, pizza restaurants and ice-cream parlours; the turrets of Callan Park Psychiatric Hospital look out across the tranquil but commercial waters of Iron Cove; and beyond the smooth curve of Rose Bay looms a convent with the grey eminence of a French fortified chateau.

I shall end my introduction to Sydney by sampling some of the districts that now contribute their individual nature to Sydney's composite character. One of the most notable of the old inner suburbs is Paddington —or "Paddo"—a coveted place to live both for its unusually pleasant atmosphere and for its conveniently central position a mile or two south-east of the harbour. It was built in the middle of the last century and for almost a hundred years was a working-class district. Many of the terrace houses on its hilly, tree-lined streets incorporate salvaged convict-made bricks, each bearing the maker's mark. After the Second World War, when Australia underwent an immigration boom, many of these then reasonably priced houses were bought or rented by the army of "New Australians" from Italy, Greece, Cyprus, Spain and many Eastern European countries. They opened local delicatessens, bakeries, fishmarkets, fruit shops and clothing stores. Many augmented their incomes by taking on extra night jobs until they could afford to buy suburban properties and put their children—the first generation of Australians in their families—through a university. "Paddo" gradually started to take on the air of an international suburb that was not quite Australian.

In the Sixties, the district underwent a further transformation; for professional people—architects, doctors, lawyers, writers, composers, artists

—"discovered" Paddington and started buying up the houses at increasingly exorbitant sums and restoring them, rediscovering the delights of inner-city living. In most cases the houses were remodelled without loss of character, but to the general comforts of the sturdy interiors was added the abundance of household machines that Australians consider to be absolute necessities.

Not all the dwellers of foreign origin moved out, so the suburb has retained an atmosphere of Europe and of Bohemianism. The houses vary from the small two-up, two-down design of late-19th-Century English terrace houses to the wider and therefore larger villas. The walls are very thick, helping to keep the inside cool in the heat. Many houses are now furnished with luxuries that would have been unthinkably far above the incomes of the original owners. At the back of each house is an enclosed garden, often with a small, brick-paved yard surrounded by citrus trees and indigenous plants.

Paddington is on the Australian National Trust's list of environmental features to be preserved. The area is liberally sprinkled with high-standard ethnic restaurants, "character" pubs where you can choose your own lunch-time steak, craftshops, coffee bars, bookshops, antique stores, old-furniture emporia, foreign-food shops and several well-established commercial art galleries. Perhaps the houses are a little too perfect now and the occupants a little too comfortable; there is a palpable sense of prosperity about the place and the cosmopolitan feeling is somewhat dimmed. But there is always movement and something going on at all hours, and the district retains something natural, some charm of place and site that is inextinguishable.

My second example of an inner-city suburb—perhaps the one I should most like to live in—is Glebe. It is a network of streets a couple of miles west of Paddington, lying between the harbour's wharfs to the north and the campus of the University of Sydney to the south. It has a fair quota of the most interesting houses in Sydney and offers many appealing glimpses: turreted silhouettes against the sky, herb gardens along delicately etched paths behind iron gates, freshly painted Italianate façades, roofs built out over the front rooms for a suggestion of shade and coolness in summer. In all, Glebe is a fine expression of the resourcefulness and restraint of Sydney's vernacular architecture. It has among its occupants a high proportion of academics and students, thanks to the proximity of the university, and manages to preserve an agreeable seediness alongside its visible prosperity.

The ideal of Sydney-living remains the house on the shore; but only a few realize this ambition. One of the easiest mistakes to make about a city that is so often viewed from the water is to believe that all its inhabitants live near the sea. But marching away from the glittering harbour into quite another world—one without the privilege of outstanding natural

Traffic at Sydney's airport funnels beneath a runway as a jet of Australia's international airline taxis above it. Flight time to London is about 24 hours.

beauty—are the miles and miles of suburbs that stretch westwards from central Sydney as far as the Blue Mountains.

The passion for home-and-garden ownership led to rapid suburban expansion during the 1930s and 1940s, and the housing estates of the far western suburbs—many of them built by private speculators—remain a striking illustration of the materialistic aspirations of less affluent Sydney-siders. Isolated agricultural townships, such as Penrith and St. Mary's, that had grown up in an earlier era, gradually became linked in one enormous conurbation, as more and more bushland was bulldozed to meet the demand for outer-city housing space. Like sprawling suburbs of any city, there is an anonymity about these vast expanses of almost treeless streets, forever repeating the pattern of red-tiled roofs and box-like homes.

The inhabitants of the western suburbs do not lack social or sporting facilities, but they are deprived of the surfing beaches and the entertainment that are easily available to dwellers in the inner-city suburbs. Unlike many other large cities, Sydney has only one real centre—and it can take as much as an hour and a half for the people of the Liverpool or Cabramatta districts to drive the 16 miles downtown in the Saturday evening traffic. Perhaps it is little wonder that the western suburbs have a higher number of violent assaults than elsewhere in Sydney and that, with the increasing wealth of the eastern and northern suburbs, there has been a rise in the rate of acquisitive crime carried out there—mainly by young men under 25 from the comparatively less well-endowed areas.

But if I had to take a biopsy of Sydney I think I would turn to quite a different world. I would attempt it in Mosman, a suburb on the north shore. Say to anyone in Australia the word Mosman and you will get the same response: Mosman is the epitome of the older sort of established, middle-class Australia. Other suburbs may be richer and have more historical associations; others may have more uncompromising problems; Mosman has Sydney's soul. It is middle-class Australia's staging post, always being left by the ambitious children of parents who overcame—but can still remember—the misery of the Depression, always being joined by new and risingly successful young couples.

Mosman is a good place to learn that politicians are human beings—or at least that their well-paid advisers are; you can meet them at parties there and hear all the scandal about Canberra, for Sydney is a city of gossip where, sooner or later, every secret is told. Mosman is where "New Australian" professional men learn to wear shorts and drink beer out of cans, and where the sons and daughters of old Australians yearn for life in Vienna or London. It is where almost everybody I know has lived at some time or another; I feel that when I die I shall have to pass through Mosman to get to heaven or hell.

Mosman is a land of banana trees and hammocks strung up in the gardens, of rambling houses—sometimes made of wood, with tiled roofs and verandas—hidden from the street by jacaranda trees. In its northern aspect it looks out on the beaches and green slopes of Middle Harbour; southwards it faces Port Jackson, where the eastern suburbs, the Opera House, Circular Quay and the Harbour Bridge are all strung out to view.

Gazing across the harbour from the wide verandas of Mosman, you can believe that Sydney is indeed Australia's great city, the answer to the pervasive provincialism that all visitors to the continent find themselves commenting upon. That provincialism was the product of Australia's long-standing cultural isolation from the rest of the Western world, cut off by distance well into the 20th Century almost as effectively as Eastern Europe is by the Iron Curtain. But today in Sydney—which boasts the continent's busiest international airport—the great silver jets come and go ceaselessly, and the "aluminium curtain" (a phrase coined in conversation by the Sydney journalist, George Munster, in 1975) can no longer prevent the city from being a metropolis of international stature.

Although Sydney may from certain angles look like Chicago, with sky-scrapers along a commercial shoreline, and its sun-filtered atmosphere may on smoggy mornings suggest Los Angeles, it is never anything but truly itself. Like any other city, it has its gasworks, its slaughterhouses, its railway yards and slums. But even they can seem touched with gentleness when, about 5 o'clock in the afternoon after a sweltering day, the southerly wind springs up and blows—not too fiercely—over the stifling city, ruffling the waters of the harbour and setting the higher leaves on the trees fluttering. At that magical time the whole, enormous, boisterous city seems both beautiful and benign.

Panorama of a Watery Labyrinth

Seen looking south, the tranquil Pacific enters Sydney Harbour between the green bluff of North Head (foreground) and the narrow tip of South Head (top, left).

Standing at the tip of Australia's eastern seaboard, Sydney sprawls like an unfinished jigsaw pattern across hundreds of interlocking headlands, bays and inlets. It is a spacious city clustered around one of the finest natural harbours in the world. From its original centre at Sydney Cove on the harbour's south shore—now the flourishing commercial district—the city has spread 35 miles inland along the labyrinth of creeks and rivers that drain into the harbour. And towards the ocean, suburbanites who love to live within sight and sound of the Pacific have colonized the serrated coastlines and the sandy beaches to the north and south of the promontories that guard the harbour mouth. Encompassing an area of some 4,650 square miles for its population of between three and four million, Sydney is as relaxed and expansive in topography as in mood.

Across the harbour from the north shore's comfortable suburbs (foreground) compactly grouped skyscrapers in the business district rise behind the curved white ro

the Opera House (top, centre). The arc of the Sydney Harbour Bridge—known affectionately as "The Coathanger"—links the north and south sides of the harbour.

Flowing under the Gladesville Bridge (centre) the Parramatta River wanders eastwards between islands and bays towards downtown Sydney and the sea. A small

...dge (left) carries a road across Tarban Creek to join the Victoria Road expressway as it sweeps from Gladesville (foreground) to Drummoyne on the south shore.

On the Pacific coast below South Head houses cling to Ben Buckler, the sandstone bluff that flanks the thousand-yard-long surfing paradise of Bondi Beach (bac

und). The jutting headland's name was bestowed by early settlers from Britain; it is a corruption of "Benbecula", one of the islands in the Scottish Hebrides.

At Sylvania Waters, on the south-west edge of Botany Bay, swampland has become an affluent area with abundant moorings along the sinuous waterfront.

Glinting in the morning light, the Pacific Ocean almost encircles Barranjoey Head and the settlement at Palm Beach, one of Sydney's far-flung northern suburbs.

2

Exiles in a Wild New World

On Sunday, May 13, 1787, eleven ships set sail from Portsmouth in England with the future population of Sydney on board. The "passenger list" included Mary Smith, 25, a dressmaker originally condemned to death for stealing "one pair of leather boots, value 21 shillings"; Thomas Josephs, also sentenced to death, for "feloniously assaulting Mary, the wife of Joseph Pullen and taking from her person one silk handkerchief, value 2 shillings"; and Thomas Chaddick, sentenced to seven years' transportation for "unlawfully, wrongfully, maliciously and injuriously" entering a private garden and plucking 12 cucumber plants. Mary Smith and Thomas Josephs had had their sentences commuted, on pleas for mercy in the light of their relatively minor offences, to a fate only slightly better than hanging: transportation to a life of hard labour in the new British penal colony being established on the shores of Botany Bay, on the newly explored south-eastern coast of Australia.

The convoy of ships, known today to every Australian as the First Fleet, carried on departure slightly more than a thousand people—759 of them convicts (including 191 women prisoners). A contingent of some 200 Royal Marines, with 19 officers, was assigned the unenviable task of guarding the convicts on the journey and acting as a "defence and discipline force" once the distant colony was established. Thirty of the marines were accompanied by their wives. Some 25 children also set out on the long journey—about half of them the offspring of the marines and the remainder the children of female convicts. Some confusion surrounds the exact number who finally arrived to become Sydney's founders and the first European settlers in Australia, since some 20 convicts died en route and several female prisoners gave birth during the eight-month voyage.

A naval officer, Captain Arthur Phillip, was put in charge of the venture and provided with extensive powers as Captain-General and Governor-in-Chief of the new territory. He proved to be a man of honesty, integrity and determination. He planned his expedition with care, and treated the convicts entrusted to him with a humane concern unusual for his day. Some of the prisoners had been loaded on to the ships, chained in pairs to the bulkheads in the holds, as long as five months before the voyage began. Phillip complained, to no avail, of the filthy clothing and squalid state in which the convicts arrived on board, and took what precautions he could to prevent illness arising from their unhygienic conditions.

Neither Phillip nor the marines knew how long they would remain in the new colony, but they could all look forward to eventual return to

The Aborigine Bennelong wears ceremonial paint in this portrait probably completed in the last decade of the 18th Century. Governor Arthur Phillip, Sydney's founder, befriended the native, using him as an interpreter; and in 1792 took him to England where, during a three-year stay, he was presented to King George III. Little is known of his life after his return to Australia, but he is thought to have died in 1813. The promontory where the city's Opera House now stands bears his name.

In this grossly idealized conception by an 18th-Century English artist, early settlers of the new British penal colony founded at Sydney Cove genteelly busy themselves building animal pens, shooting game birds, capturing turtles and dominating the Aborigines. In reality the colonists—officers and troops as well as the convicts—led a life of squalor and severe hardship in the settlement's first years.

England when their terms of service were over. The convicts, on the other hand, were unlikely ever to make their way back, even after serving their sentences. The British government had no intention of providing transport for them; and it was unlikely they would ever be able to afford the price of the voyage back, should any ship accept them as paying passengers. In fact, one advocate of establishing a penal colony in Australia had openly argued that its distance from England would mean that the homeland would be rid of these undesirables forever.

What was to become of these exiles when they were freed? The British government gave Phillip the right to make land grants to reformed convicts —and to any marines who wished to retire in the new settlement. Beyond that, the matter does not seem to have been given much consideration. The government's main concern was to get an unwanted burden out of sight and mind by relieving the pressure on its overcrowded jails, crammed beyond capacity as a result of far-reaching economic and political changes. For, in Britain, the urbanization and social upheavals of the Industrial Revolution had given rise to an increasingly crime-prone city population; while in America the British colonies' Declaration of Independence in 1776 meant that these regions could no longer be used, as they had been before, as a dumping ground for excess convicts.

The English explorer, Captain James Cook, had visited Botany Bay 18 years earlier, in 1770, and the idea began to take hold with the British Home Secretary, Lord Sydney, and others, that Australia might be just the place to send British felons. Cook, in H.M.S. *Endeavour*, had charted almost the entire eastern coast of Australia, claiming the land in the name of George III. He named Botany Bay after the great number of exotic plants collected there by gentleman-botanist Joseph Banks, who accompanied him on the voyage. Cook wrote in his diary that the place was endowed with "a deep black soil" and "as fine meadow as ever was seen".

Cook's observations convinced officials in London that the convicts would be able to grow enough food to feed themselves. The area might also become a safe supplier of tall timber for ships' masts and flax for sails. Further, the British were anxious lest their enemies the French should show an interest in what might become a valuable strategic territory. However, officials in London were clear on one point: the colony was to be a penal settlement and nothing more. The British government was to be responsible for running it and for any trade it generated. The government calculated that it would need to supply, at the taxpayers' expense, all the colony's requirements for the first year, and half of them for the second and third years. After that it was to become self-supporting.

Fortunately for the future city of Sydney, Phillip was a man of vision, whose view of the colony's possibilities was somewhat different from that of his superiors. He wished to found a colony that would flourish and endure. It was with such lofty thoughts that he weighed anchor and set sail

for Australia with his shabby cargo of convicts. During the long journey small groups of prisoners, under guard and on a rotation basis, were allowed on deck without chains in the sunshine and fresh air. But not all of the officers held Phillip's humanitarian convictions: records show that numerous prisoners were flogged for relatively minor offences.

The fleet followed the time-honoured route to the Pacific in those early pre-Suez Canal days: south-west from England to Rio de Janeiro in South America (where the ships remained for a month taking on supplies), then south-east to the Cape of Good Hope on Africa's southern tip (another month's stop), and finally the 7,000-mile lap to Australia. Phillip's own ship, H.M.S. *Sirius*, arrived a few days before the others, putting in at Botany Bay on January 18, 1788. The first of the convicts were unloaded at the site that was finally selected—a stone's throw from what is now downtown Sydney—on the historic date of January 26.

Few great cities have such a short and dramatic history as Sydney—or such a starkly etched birthdate. It is a peculiar feeling to know that your city, and country, began on one fine day; or on "one finite date" might be a better way of putting it. Australia cannot claim the kind of proud myth that every country seems to need. Sydney did not begin as a trading post or the site of a previous civilization; no god guided its founders and no star hovered over it. There are only the brutal facts of the convict expedition.

In spite of—or perhaps because of—this quick rise from a questionable start, Sydney people seem to have a lust for history, a hardly-to-be-slaked thirst for facts and stories about their origins. Australian history has become a big domestic business; academic books and popular accounts tumble from the presses in greater numbers as the pursuit of historical roots accelerates. In modern commercial Sydney, some of the most flourishing shops are devoted to Australiana—the stuff sold varies from tea-towels with Aboriginal motifs to expensive facsimiles of early colonial scenes and documents. If you look hard enough, you can pick up an appropriate icon for every major event, from the settling of the convict colony in 1788 to the first performance at the Opera House in 1973.

Naturally, theories abound as to how the convicts may have shaped the personality of the present city. John Pringle, an Englishman who served as editor of the *Sydney Morning Herald* in the 1950s writes: "Deep in the secret heart of Sydney, beneath the brashness and the pride and the boasting, is a memory of human suffering, and a resentment against those who caused it." Yet historian Sir Keith Hancock concludes: "All the clues which seem at first sight to suggest the visible and persistent influence of convictism upon Australian life prove in the end to be misleading."

One descendant of the early settlers with a strong—and positive—opinion about the influence of the convict past has been Jonathan King, whose ancestor, Philip Gidley King, arrived in Australia as a naval

Landmarks of Hard-Earned Success

B.C.c.30000		Nomadic hunter-gatherers, forebears of modern Aborigines, migrate from South-East Asia into Australian continent via a prehistoric land-link
A.D.	1605	Dutch merchant ship makes first documented European sighting of Australia's north-east coast
	1642	Dutch explorer Abel Tasman discovers an island off south-east Australia, later named Tasmania
	1699	English buccaneer William Dampier charts Australia's north-west coast for the British Admiralty
	1770	James Cook, English naval explorer, claims eastern half of Australia for the British Crown, naming it New South Wales (N.S.W.). He lands at Botany Bay, but sails past mouth of Sydney Harbour without entering
	1788	British settlers of the First Fleet—marines and convicts under command of Captain Arthur Phillip—establish penal colony at Sydney Cove
	1789	Phillip initiates grants of land to marines and emancipated convicts as well. Second Fleet arrives with much-needed supplies
	1792	Phillip returns to England because of failing health. Settlement's population numbers 3,500, some three-quarters of them convicts
1792-1809		Officers of the military garrison led by Captain John Macarthur operate lucrative monopoly in rum—important as a commodity for bartering. Known as the Rum Corps, they become the effective rulers of the colony
	1804	Concerted uprising by 400 rebellious Irish convicts is suppressed. Sheep farming begins with stock brought from England
	1806	William Bligh, previously captain of H.M.S. "Bounty", appointed Governor of New South Wales
	1808	Bligh arrests Rum Corps leader Macarthur in attempt to break the trade monopoly, but is himself seized by rebel officers and held prisoner for a year
	1809	Bligh replaced by Governor Lachlan Macquarie, who arrives with a British regiment and disbands the Rum Corps, re-establishing law and order
	1810	Population of New South Wales totals 10,000
	1813	Australian-born explorer William Wentworth and two companions make first trek across the Blue Mountains, 50 miles west of Sydney, discovering extensive grasslands ideal for sheep rearing
	1820s	Frontiersmen establish communities west of the Blue Mountains, dispossessing the semi-nomadic Aborigines, a thinly spread population numbering about 300,000 over the whole continent
	1822	Macquarie resigns after British government criticism of his policies: expensive construction of roads and public buildings, and emancipation of convicts
	1823	Inauguration of first legislative council of New South Wales, a body of up to seven members with purely advisory powers, appointed by the governor
	1824	First independent newspaper, "The Australian", published by Wentworth, who campaigns for the political and legal rights of emancipated convicts and their descendants
	1828	Legislative council enlarged to 15 members, with extended powers to defeat governor's measures
	1832	To encourage settlement of Australia, British government subsidizes travel costs of emigrants. Over next 10 years, some 70,000 arrive at Sydney
	1840	Transportation of convicts to New South Wales ends
	1842	Legislative council enlarged to 36 members, 12 still nominated by the governor but 24 elected by citizens
	1844	Semicircular Quay (later abbreviated to Circular Quay) completed at Sydney Cove
	1850	Wool exported from Sydney accounts for more than 40 per cent of British wool imports. The Australian Colonies Government Act establishes partially self-governing colonies in Tasmania, Victoria and South Australia
	1851	A gold rush following several strikes near Sydney and Melbourne leads to surge of immigration: Sydney's population increases in 10 years from 54,000 to 96,000

lieutenant with the First Fleet and eventually went on to become the colony's third Governor. A political science lecturer at Melbourne University and the author of four history books, Jonathan King identified for me several traits that are remnants of the city's convict heritage. "There's a strain of irreverence in the modern Sydneysider," he observed. "People see today's figures of authority rather as the convicts saw their guards. There's also a conviction that Jack is as good as his master. In a society where people pulled themselves up from such a bad start, no one has a right to say he's better than the next man."

Why are Sydneysiders so history mad? "What other society started off in chains?" King asked. "We're proud of what we made of Australia. And people love to read about how it happened. It's an exciting, dramatic and romantic story. And it all began just yesterday. You can get hold of it; you can always see back to the starting-point."

King's own illustrious ancestor was indeed there at the starting-point; his diary—now in the Mitchell Library in Sydney—is one of the treasured documents that helps to record how it all began. Entries in it for the first few days after the arrival at Botany Bay reflect relief that the voyage was over but also record a major disappointment. Cook's meadow and fine soil were nowhere to be found—and to this day it remains unclear why the normally meticulous Captain apparently blundered. King explored the land around Botany Bay with Governor Phillip and wrote in his diary that he found "the country low and boggy" with "no appearance of fresh water".

It took Governor Phillip only a few days to conclude that Botany Bay was unsuitable for settlement. A man of initiative, he set out to explore the next harbour to the north, named Port Jackson by Cook, after Second Secretary of the Admiralty and family friend George Jackson. Cook had sailed past its apparently slight entrance without investigating it. "We got into Port Jackson early in the afternoon," Phillip later wrote to Lord Sydney, in his first dispatch, in phrases that have since become famous, "and had the satisfaction of finding the finest harbour in the world, in which a thousand sail of the line may ride in the most perfect security." The cove that he selected for settlement, he added diplomatically, "I honoured with the name of Sydney". The name stuck, for the colony as well as the cove, although Phillip had intended to call the settlement Albion.

Phillip's choice of the cove was dictated by the presence of a stream of potable fresh water that entered the sea there. This once sparkling rivulet —prosaically called the Tank Stream by the settlers, after the sandstone tanks they built to store the water—has now been confined to a concrete pipe that runs through the foundations of the Stock Exchange Centre. If you stop in the centre's underground car park you are actually beneath the historic flow of water that helped to determine the site of the city.

January 26 is now designated as Australia Day. Each year to celebrate the anniversary of 1788, a few modern Sydneysiders don historic costumes and re-enact the landing. They do not, however, re-enact what happened some two weeks later, when about a hundred of the women convicts were landed from the *Lady Penrhyn*. Arthur Bowes, one of the ship's surgeons, wrote in his diary: "The men convicts got to them very soon after they landed, and it is beyond my abilities to give a just description of the scene of debauchery and riot that ensued during the night." Shortly after the landing "there came on the most violent storm of thunder, lightening [*sic*] and rain I ever saw," Bowes continued. But the revelries went on, "some swearing, others quarrelling, others singing— not in the least regarding the tempest".

Order was slowly established, but most of the convicts remained unenthusiastic settlers. Some escaped into the bush, believing that China was a short overland journey away; a number of these were never seen again and presumably died in the wilderness; others eventually returned to the colony rather than face the inhospitable bush country.

Among the convicts were a few trained carpenters and bricklayers, but many had no useful trade or skill. Stealing and drunkenness were therefore common and punishments severe; convicts and marines alike received up to 500 lashes, or were put to death, for their crimes. One of Phillip's officers, Captain Watkin Tench, recorded in his diary that the convicts "behaved better than had been predicted of them—to have expected sudden and complete reformation of conduct were romantic and chimerical". Some contemporary diaries read more like a police gazette than the record of the beginning of a noble civilization. In another, the entry for Christmas Eve, 1788, states: "Amelia Levy and Elizabeth Fowles spent the night with Corporal Plowman and Corporal Winxstead in return for a shirt each."

Although Port Jackson was preferable to Botany Bay, the setting was far from ideal. Rocky promontories, sandy beaches, outcrops of stone, beautiful but unproductive shrubs—all of these may be the perfect background for a modern picnic; but to a band of desperate men and women with few provisions, 12,000 miles from home, the unwelcoming and barren scene must have been appalling.

Wrote Captain Tench: "The dread of want in a country destitute of natural resources is ever peculiarly terrible," and "the possession of a spade, a wheelbarrow or a dunghill, was more coveted than the most refulgent arms in which heroism ever dazzled." The soil was so stony it broke tools; the trees cut down for lumber turned out to be either too hard or too brittle for efficient use in constructing houses; some of the seeds brought from Cape Town when the First Fleet stopped there on the way had spoilt on the journey and would not sprout, and of those that survived, a disproportionate number were devoured by pests.

The officers had joked as pairs of goats, sheep and cattle were loaded on board at Cape Town that their expedition was another Noah's Ark.

A bewigged Sydneysider representing Governor Phillip scans the coast with a telescope during the annual re-enactment of the landing in 1788 by Australia's first European colonists: an advance party of marines and seamen from the First Fleet of 11 British ships. The Australia Day celebration takes place each year on the Sunday nearest to January 26, the date of Phillip's disembarkation at Sydney Cove.

However, after the landing, most of the livestock were secretly butchered for food or disappeared into the bush, and thus never multiplied as intended. An exception was a group of cattle that wandered off and was found years later with offspring in a place some 30 miles from the original settlement. In an area now within commuting distance on Sydney's city limits there is a highway called Cowpasture Road.

Few of the convicts had any agricultural knowledge or experience to contribute to the colony's attempts to grow food. Rations were cut and cut again, and Captain Tench reported "If a lucky man, who had knocked down a dinner with his gun, or caught a fish by angling from the rocks, invited a neighbour to dine with him, the invitation always ran 'bring your own bread'. Even at the Governor's table, this custom was constantly observed. Every man when he sat down pulled his bread out of his pocket, and laid it by his plate."

As the months grew into a year, and then two years, with no mail or news from home, many convicts and officers alike became convinced that the colony had been abandoned to eventual extinction, and that the land would revert to the Aborigines who had inhabited it for thousands of years before their arrival. The Aborigines' way of life, so different from that of the white settlers, had allowed them to exist in harmony with an environment that had brought the Europeans to the verge of starvation.

In fact, the area around Sydney Cove was much more abundant in food than many of the places where the Aborigines managed to survive. Fish was plentiful and so was game, such as kangaroo, and these formed a large part of the diet of the Aborigines in the Port Jackson region. They also ate wild honey, yams, birds' eggs, berries, water-lily roots, lizards, rats and insects. The secret of the Aborigines' way of life was migration— they did not farm, but travelled nomadically in small groups, returning to places only after supplies had been naturally replenished.

When the Europeans arrived, at least four different Aboriginal tribes were living in the Port Jackson area, each with a somewhat different language. The historian Geoffrey Blainey says: "The language spoken on the site of the present Opera House was not spoken on the facing shore. An Aboriginal paddling his canoe across to the north shore had to speak not merely in a different dialect but a different language." A few Aboriginal words survive in Sydney place-names, though most have been corrupted by the white Australians' pronunciation. Three of the area's beaches, for instance, were named after their attributes. Bondi, from *boondi*—sound of thundering water; Cronulla, from *kurranulla*—small pink shells; and Coogee, from *koocha*—the smell of rotting seaweed.

Lieutenant King's diary entry describing one of the first meetings between the settlers and Aborigines reflects the innocence of the early encounters. His exploration party had met a group of native men and offered them presents. "They wanted to know what sex we were," he writes, "which they explained by pointing to where it was distinguishable. As they took us for women, not having our beard grown, I ordered one of the people to undeceive them in this particular, when they made a great shout of admiration. . . ." Soon Aborigine women and girls appeared too, and King wrote, "Those natives who were round the boats made signs for us to go to them and made us understand their persons were at our service. However, I declined this mark of their hospitality but showed a handkerchief, which I offered to one of the women, pointing her out. She immediately put her child down and came alongside the boat and suffered me to apply the handkerchief where Eve did the fig leaf. . . ." As his descendant, Jonathan King, remarked, "He must have been an extra-ordinarily serious man. The natives had been wandering around happily without clothes for thousands of years, yet he was anxious to show them what, to his mind, was right—and on the very first day on shore."

But various episodes of misunderstanding and conflict soon complicated the settlers' relations with the Aborigines, whose occasional hostility thereafter contributed to the insecurity of the colony. The Aborigines never attacked the settlement at Sydney, but two convicts cutting rushes were killed in the May of 1788 and, in March of the next year, a party of convicts heading for an Aboriginal camp to steal the natives' fishing tackle and spears, were ambushed by a group of Aborigines who suspected their intentions; one of the convicts was killed and several wounded.

With worries about the Aborigines, food shortages growing daily more severe and a work-force of recalcitrant convicts, Phillip was anxious to get

Oxen haul an empty cart up Brickfield Hill in 1796. This area of claypits, located one mile south of Sydney Cove and now part of the central city, provided materials for convict-made bricks used in the construction of the colony's first buildings. In the earliest years of the settlement, before draught animals were imported, the carts—each loaded with more than 300 bricks —were manhandled up the hill by teams of 12 convicts, urged on by a whip-wielding overseer.

supplies and reinforcements from home. But this shabby penal settlement in the Pacific was certainly not the British government's first priority. To make matters worse, one relief ship dispatched to the colony hit an iceberg and never arrived. The first ship from Britain carrying food, equipment and more convicts did not arrive until two and a half years after the original settlers had landed.

Several other vessels soon followed, bringing to the settlers the much-needed psychological reassurance that they were not forgotten, as well as renewing their stores of staple foods and the manufactured goods that they could not provide for themselves. The colony at last began to make headway and its survival was soon assured. By 1791 a hospital, barracks and three government warehouses had been erected, and the colony's much-encouraged gardens were producing a modest supply of fruit and vegetables. Some of the marines had already chosen to retire in the growing settlement, but most were becoming restive after more than three years in the distant colony. When Phillip, for reasons of health, sailed for home at the end of 1792, marines wishing to return were withdrawn with him and replaced by a newly constituted military force, the New South Wales Corps. By this time, Sydney was a solid, albeit harsh, reality.

For 20th-Century Sydneysiders, the records of the early days—with their nightmare intensity and peculiar drabness of narrative—are both fascinating and difficult to project. Thus, thousands flock at weekends to Old Sydney Town, a reconstruction of the settlement as it was around

Lace Crafted in Iron

Sydney's rapid expansion during the 19th Century coincided with increasing interest in a versatile building material: ornamental cast iron. The city's equable climate favoured housing with cool balconies and verandas; and cast-iron work—delicate in appearance, yet very strong—was uniquely suited to their construction. It provided privacy, shade and abundant variety for rows of otherwise almost identical two-storey houses in suburbs such as Glebe and Paddington (*overpage*).

The city's first home-produced metalwork, cast in the 1840s from pig-iron imported from England, at first followed restrained Georgian designs. But local taste soon demanded a more florid style, and new iron-work patterns became ever more elaborate. The selection illustrated here includes designs reflecting the exuberance of Australian plants and birds—such as ferns (*top row, left*) and the tails of lyre-birds (*bottom row, left*).

Carefully renovated terraces of small, 19th-Century houses, many with cast-iron balconies, bring a harmony of style to the sloping, tree-lined streets of the inner-city suburb of Paddington—affectionately known as "Paddo". Inhabited during the 1940s predominantly by low-income families and immigrants, the neighbourhood has since become a fashionable artistic quarter whose village-like charm is protected by an active preservation society.

1800, built on the shores of an artificial lake 50 miles north of the city. There, Sydneysiders can board a replica of a brigantine, stroll down the few streets of the sanitized old town, and inspect craftsmen's shops, a barracks and, inevitably, a jail and punishment yard.

In the slightly Disneyland atmosphere of Old Sydney Town, the simplified facts of the first settlement are drawn with comic-strip emphasis. On the day I visited, the most popular entertainment was the 2 p.m. public "flogging", and the highlight of this unedifying spectacle was a re-enactment of the whipping of a female prisoner. (I was startled by the number of visitors speaking very imperfect English. I appreciated at length that these were recent immigrants from such diverse countries as Italy, Yugoslavia and Lebanon on a crash course in the history of their adopted land.) Native Australians appear to find the place very *déjà vu*; but it is, after all, a testimony to the ultimate success of their city. Despite the garishness of the exhibition, you do come away reflecting on the achievements of the men and women who turned this brutally inauspicious beginning into today's thriving metropolis.

Although the early days of near starvation were followed by a period of relative prosperity and growth, the course from penal colony to commercial giant did not run smoothly. In fact, the 15 years following Phillip's departure were marked by raging controversies that developed between the different interest groups in the artificially closed and isolated society of the settlement.

As the eventual third Governor, Philip Gidley King was deeply involved in the feuding. His problem was the army. Recruited from the residue of the British Army—all the best troops and officers were fully engaged in fighting the Napoleonic Wars—the New South Wales Corps was a somewhat disreputable security force for the colony. No governor had been appointed for three years after Phillip's departure and in the interim the military ran things to their own advantage. A Major Grose was made Acting Governor; and when permission was received from London to grant land to officers serving in the military—a request made earlier by Governor Phillip—Grose showed no restraint, allotting fellow officers large parcels of land with a heedlessness that accounts to this day for many of the strange twists and turns of Sydney's streets. He also provided the officers with free convict labour and, even more important, allowed them to establish a near monopoly over trade. Commerce was inhibited by lack of currency, since the colonists could not mint their own, and barter was the common form of trading. Many officers made fortunes in one particular commodity: rum. The New South Wales Corps soon came to be known, appropriately, as the Rum Corps.

When the colony's second Governor, John Hunter, finally did arrive in 1795, the Rum Corps, accustomed to having its own way, made his life difficult by its insubordination. He complained to the Home Secretary, but London had no time for what appeared to be an ineffective Governor. In 1799 he was recalled. When King succeeded Hunter in September 1800, he was faced with cleaning up the army and found himself in conflict with the Rum Corps's unofficial head, Captain John Macarthur. King dubbed Macarthur "the Perturbator"; another contemporary said of Macarthur that he was "as sharp as a razor and as rapacious as a shark". Historians have had a harder time assessing the man, since he is both a hero and a villain in the saga of the country's growth.

While Macarthur's participation in the rum trade is highly discreditable, his work in animal husbandry is difficult to fault. He founded one of the first efficient farms in the colony; Elizabeth Farm (named after his wife) near what is now the Sydney suburb of Parramatta, is today preserved as part of the nation's heritage. On it he crossbred the spindly English sheep, whose virtue was their hardiness and endurance, with the abundantly coated Spanish merino, and thereby helped lay the foundation for the Australian wool industry. On the other hand, he was in constant conflict with King, who was attempting to force the military out of the rum trade. In 1802, when Macarthur wounded his commanding officer, Colonel Paterson, in a duel (fought because Paterson would not join a boycott of King organized by Macarthur), King at last had a good reason to be rid of him. The Governor sent him off to England to face a court martial.

Although thus freed of Macarthur, King still faced other immediate problems. In March 1804 some 400 convicts staged the first and only convict uprising in the history of the colony. Its leaders were drawn from a group of Irish political offenders who had been transported to Australia following the rebellion of 1798. In the fighting, which lasted less than a day, 15 convicts were killed. Eight of their leaders were later hanged.

King had barely recovered from the shock of the episode, when who should reappear on the scene but the Perturbator himself. He had managed to avoid court martial in Britain on a technical point concerning whether Sydney or London was the correct location for such a trial. Macarthur counted among his friends people in high places in London and through them had been introduced to some of Britain's most eminent wool manufacturers, whom he impressed with the quality of his wool samples. Provided with financial and political backing by the textile tycoons and his influential friends, he resigned his army commission to return to Sydney in 1805 with a grant from the British government of 5,000 acres of land and some prize merinos from George III's personal flocks. Following Macarthur's triumphant return, King had little hope of breaking the power of the Rum Corps; in 1806 he was recalled to London, where he died two years later.

After King's death, his wife and son returned to Australia. The boy, Phillip Parker King, grew up to become the first Australian-born admiral in the British Navy, known primarily for his work in charting the continent's northern coast. One of Phillip Parker King's sons sailed with Darwin on H.M.S. *Beagle*, and returned to a political career in Sydney. The third Governor's descendants also include bankers, several government officials, an oilman—and historian Jonathan King.

By now London was aware that a strong man was needed to govern Sydney and thought it had just the person: William Bligh, the same man who had survived the mutiny on H.M.S. *Bounty* 17 years earlier, in April 1789. Serious historians have been kinder to Bligh than popular writers and Hollywood, assessing him not as a paranoid autocrat but as a resourceful and intelligent man. But there is no disagreement on one point: he had a hot temper. When Bligh, attempting to break the trade monopoly, collided with Macarthur, the explosion was spectacular. Macarthur found himself in jail under arrest on a variety of charges, including vilifying the Governor. But the acting commandant of the New South Wales Corps, Major George Johnston, freed him and, on a hot summer night in 1808, the Rum Corps rebelled, arrested Bligh and took over the rule of the colony.

Bligh was kept under house arrest for more than a year and then placed aboard H.M.S. *Porpoise* bound for England. No sooner was he at sea than he reasserted his commission as Governor and declared the colony to be officially in a state of rebellion. But, helpless to do anything about it, he proceeded southward to Hobart, the new capital of the island of Tasmania, which—partly as a result of Sydney's progress—had in 1803 also been settled as a penal colony.

The British government, still at war with Napoleon, was somewhat bewildered by these events in Sydney. It was, however, at last convinced that the Rum Corps had to be disbanded. In 1809, yet another new Governor, Lieutenant-Colonel Lachlan Macquarie, was sent to Sydney with the regiment he commanded—the 73rd Foot—to replace the New South Wales Corps. Macquarie was ordered to arrest Major Johnston— and Macarthur as well, if there were evidence he was behind the rebellion.

But when the new Governor arrived, both men had already departed for London to argue their case there. (Johnston was eventually court-martialled, but allowed to return to his extensive farm in Sydney. Macarthur remained in London for several years until the trouble blew over, then returned to his merinos.) Some members of the New South Wales Corps were accepted into Macquarie's regiment and eventually retired in Sydney, but more than half returned to London. Before taking office himself, Macquarie had orders to reinstate Bligh as Governor for a day, but Bligh did not arrive from Hobart in time to be symbolically reinstated. On his return to London, Bligh was eventually promoted to rear-admiral, but never again held such great responsibilities.

Macquarie was a Scotsman devoted to duty and order and, in his dozen years as Governor, he left his mark indelibly on Sydney. His influence is

A Sydneysider slowly conquers the steep hill leading past The Hero of Waterloo Hotel, one of Australia's oldest inns. Situated in The Rocks, an historic district west of Sydney Cove, the hostelry was granted its licence in 1845. The iron brackets over the door supported a gas lamp, required by law to guide travellers at night.

attested by the frequency with which his name, and the names of his family, recur in New South Wales: on streets, capes, rivers, a university, and even a sandstone resting spot, on a promontory near the Opera House, known as Mrs. Macquarie's Chair.

With the help of a gifted architect named Francis Greenway—who was transported to Australia for forgery and who today has his image engraved on Australia's $10 bill—Macquarie began to design a city with churches, hospitals, schools and court-houses. Greenway's simple, elegant and beautifully proportioned buildings are still among the most admired in Sydney. Many of them have, in fact, been elevated in modern times to more prestigious purposes; his convict barracks in Hyde Park now house the district law courts and his stables for Government House have been converted for use by the Conservatorium of Music.

Macquarie was interested in improving not only the city's physical appearance, but also its inhabitants' morals. He encouraged marriage (it has been estimated that at the time of his arrival two-thirds of the children in Sydney were illegitimate). He attempted to curb the heavy consumption of alcohol by reducing the number of pubs and shops selling liquor. To raise morale and fill out the social calendar, he had an elegant racecourse laid out and organized cricket matches and an annual Governor's ball.

In his attempts to reorganize the colony's social relations, however, Macquarie ran into trouble with the Exclusionists, the handful of free settlers and retired army officers who saw themselves as Sydney's aristocracy. Macquarie's offence was in attempting to grant social recognition to former convicts, known in Sydney as the Emancipists. He not only invited rehabilitated convicts to dinners at the Governor's mansion, he even began to appoint them to public office. When John Macarthur, at that time still in London, heard of these developments from his wife at home in Sydney, he replied, "God alone knows how such a state of things as you describe may terminate. . . ."

Despite the social pressures against them, a number of former convicts scored remarkable successes. George Barrington—who, in his former life, had earned the title "King of the Pickpockets"—was transported to Sydney in 1791 and, five years later, became Chief of Police in Parramatta; William Redfern, a doctor exiled for political offences, rose to such a high social and financial standing in the colony due to his skill as a surgeon and success as a landholder that he was appointed a director of the Bank of New South Wales; Michael Robinson, transported for blackmail in 1796, made a reputation as a poet; Mary Reibey, convicted for horse-stealing at the age of 13, became a successful merchant-trader; and Simeon Lord, locked up for stealing several lengths of fabric, made a fortune by setting up factories to produce wool cloth, hats, shoes, blankets, soap and candles.

Young William Charles Wentworth, whose mother was a convict and father a surgeon of uncertain repute who came to Sydney with the First

During an outbreak of bubonic plague in 1900, dead rats lie heaped at the feet of professional rat-catchers employed by the city of Sydney to control the disease-carrying vermin. The eight-month epidemic drew attention to severe overcrowding and lack of sanitation in a city where the population—boosted particularly by the gold rush of the 1850s—had soared in half a century from 50,000 to 196,000.

Fleet, made a name for himself as an explorer during Macquarie's term of office and went on to a brilliant career as a journalist and politician. He is now known as "the father of the Australian Constitution" for his work in obtaining a representative legislature for New South Wales. In spite of his outstanding contribution, Wentworth—who died in 1872—was snubbed all his life by the Exclusionists. If he were alive today, would he be treated any differently? The answer, it is increasingly evident, is yes; it has become trendy and fashionable to have a convict ancestor. The stigma associated with convict origins largely disappeared in the 1970s, to be replaced by a swelling pride in the achievements of the early settlers in the face of tremendous obstacles.

Macquarie was clearly far ahead of his time in his support for the Emancipists. But he had another large problem. His expenditure for roads and buildings caused raised eyebrows back in London, where funds were still short after the huge expenses incurred by the Napoleonic Wars. A commissioner was therefore dispatched to assess developments in Sydney. His official reports severely criticized Macquarie for his building programme and liberal attitude toward former convicts, and eventually led to Macquarie's resignation. But the commissioner made one important recommendation: that "persons of respectability" be encouraged, by grants of land, to settle in Sydney to expand the wool industry, so that New South Wales might more quickly evolve into a profitable colony.

A completely unrelated event made these recommendations particularly timely. In 1813 William Charles Wentworth, Gregory Blaxland and

William Lawson teamed up to find a route across the Blue Mountains, whose 3,000-foot-high chain 50 miles west of Sydney had until then proved a barrier to expansion inland from the eastern coastal plain. On the other side of the range the three men discovered rich grasslands that were perfect for rearing merino sheep.

Pioneers soon followed in the footsteps of the explorers, starting by planting settlements in the stretch between Sydney and the Blue Mountains, and later colonizing the grasslands beyond the range. Taking the line of least resistance, these men and women usually travelled up the courses of the rivers and creeks that eventually drain into Sydney Harbour, and the nearest of the settlements they founded have since become the nuclei for modern Sydney's outer suburbs.

It is a poignant experience to leave the commercial bustle of Sydney today and drive into the immediate hinterland, tracing the directions the early settlers took as they pushed beyond the city. Once, driving with a friend past the little village of Wiseman's Ferry, 48 miles north of the city centre, and along the McDonald River (a tributary of the Hawkesbury), I stopped to admire a beautiful expanse of lily-covered water on which a dozen black swans floated. My friend knew of an old graveyard nearby, which we located on spotting a few iron rails, that had once served as a fence, trailing into the undergrowth. The headstones, when they could be deciphered, surprisingly yielded not English names but those of German families—a necessary reminder to me that, almost from the start, the British settlers had been joined by a few isolated communities of religious iconoclasts from other European countries, who were at odds with authorities at home. The numbers were small, however; most groups seeking religious freedom migrated to the Americas, since the journey from Europe was shorter, and more tempting opportunities beckoned. As late as 1914, only 3 per cent of Australia's population was of non-British stock, and Australians still saw themselves as a nation of transplanted Britons. Not until after the Second World War was the balance altered by the arrival of large numbers of immigrants, especially from Greece, Yugoslavia and Lebanon.

As the number of free settlers grew, the frontier moved further west. Sydney was still kingpin of the continent, but it was no longer Australia's only town. By 1830, the settlements of Bathurst and Orange had been established some hundred miles from Sydney beyond the Blue Mountains. Brisbane, 460 miles up the coast to the north, was founded as a "maximum security" penal settlement for Sydney's really hard cases. Melbourne, 430 miles to the south-west, was founded by wool colonists, but later also received consignments of transported convicts. Perth, on the distant western seaboard, and Adelaide, now the capital of South Australia State, were both established by free colonists. Perth later received some convicts, but Adelaide never did, a fact its residents are proud of to this day.

From the 1830s onwards, Sydney was to be jolted in new directions by movements and events that often had their major impact somewhere else. One of the main stimuli was the expanding wool industry. Wool production had its base in the grazing lands beyond Sydney, but its effect on the city itself was profound. In wool, the colony finally had a money-making export, and wealth from the wool industry brought prosperity not only to Sydney but to the countryside as well.

The wool business also attracted ambitious new settlers and, to lighten the burden of overcrowding in cities in the United Kingdom, the British government added an incentive by offering to pay a good part of the fare of any person interested in emigrating. So as to balance the sexes (men are estimated to have outnumbered women by three to one in Sydney in 1830), unmarried women were especially sought. Notices advertising the opportunities—and the fact that most of the cost of the passage would be met by the government—were posted in England's cities, and ships were hired "especially for the conveyance of female emigrants". Between 1834 and 1845 more than 70,000 free immigrants arrived in New South Wales—and helped to reinforce the settlement's desire to free itself of the odium of being a penal colony.

One visitor to Sydney who commented on the original worm-within-the-bud of the proud new colony was Charles Darwin. After his historic voyage to South America and to the Galapagos Islands in the *Beagle*, Darwin put in at Sydney in 1836 on his way back to England. He took an instant dislike to Sydney society, empathizing with the native life—animal and human—and deploring the havoc wreaked on it by the settlers, their dogs, their pastimes (such as unrestrained hunting) and the diseases that they carried with them. What upset him most was the exploitation of convict labour; he felt it odious "to be waited on by a man who the day before, perhaps, was flogged for some trifling misdemeanour" and had no redress. His parting words were: "Farewell, Australia! You are a rising child. But you are too great and ambitious for affection, yet not great enough for respect. I leave your shores without sorrow or regret."

In 1840 convict transportation to New South Wales was halted, although traffic in British felons to other parts of Australia continued until 1868. Certainly a growing sense of the injustice of the convicts' fate helped stop it; but also many people in Britain were beginning to think that transportation wasn't bad enough. What sort of punishment was it, they asked, "to be carried to a country where the climate is delightful" eventually to "become a settler on a fertile farm" that could be passed on to one's children?

By the end of the convict era, Sydney had already formed a new identity as the chief Australian port of the wool trade and the location of the colony's main wool market. Newly arrived settlers were advised to "put their money in four legs". They headed across the Blue Mountains in search of an unoccupied tract to use as a sheep-run. The land officially belonged to the Crown; the new arrivals simply "squatted" on it—a practice that came to be considered more respectable as the squatters' wealth grew. Soon the squatters—some of whom took over tens and even hundreds of thousands of acres—had become wool kings and were building town mansions in Sydney. Eventually they won the right to own the land. By the mid-19th Century their power was so great that New South Wales was said to be run by a "squatocracy".

The demand for more grazing land was the main impetus for exploration of the still-mysterious interior of the continent—a quest that spanned the decades between 1840 and 1860. Search expeditions set off from Sydney and other centres, and the towns waited anxiously for news of the explorers' finds. For all the much-publicized competitiveness and will-to-win of modern Australians, it seems, paradoxically, that the most admired Australian explorers are those who set off into the outback never to return. The mystery of their fate especially endears these men to Sydneysiders.

Ludwig Leichhardt, a German-born scientist who vanished in 1848 in an attempt to be the first to cross the continent east to west on a 2,000-mile trek from near Brisbane to Perth, has a Sydney suburb named after him—now largely inhabited, incongruously, by the families of later Italian immigrants. I single out his legend from among many because it seems to have inspired Sydney's most famous author, Nobel prize-winner Patrick White, to write his novel *Voss*, which tells the story of a doomed

Crowds gather in Sydney's Centennial Park on January 1, 1901, to watch the ceremonial inauguration of the first Governor-General of the new Commonwealth of Australia: a federation of the six Australian colonies of New South Wales, Victoria, South Australia, Tasmania, Western Australia and Queensland. Sydney's efforts to become the federal capital—strongly opposed by Melbourne, the capital of Victoria—failed; as a compromise, a new capital was created at Canberra, a settlement whose name derives from an Aboriginal word for "meeting-place".

voyager's journey into the drought-stricken outback—and into the equally hazardous symbolic Freudian badlands of the human mind.

Grasslands were opened up in various regions, but in the heart of the continent the explorers discovered little fertile land. The interior turned out to be a vast and barren desert, lacking the inland sea that many early settlers were convinced lay somewhere out there.

While the explorers were tramping across the outback, steps towards responsible government were being taken in Sydney. In 1823, a legislative council of five to seven members had been established with the power to make laws for the peace, welfare and good government of the colony. All members were appointed by the governor, who could, on London's approval, override any decision the council made. In 1842 the council was enlarged, with two-thirds of its 36 members elected by a small body of voters, mainly owners of extensive properties.

A constitution was next on the agenda. It took several years to draft, and several more to get the British government's approval, but was finally accepted in 1855. It provided for an upper house of 21 members nominated by the governor, and a legislative assembly of 54 members chosen on a liberal franchise. By 1860 all men had the vote and New South Wales's first Parliament had been convened. (Women got the vote in 1902—long before British women were fully enfranchised in 1928.)

A visitor to Sydney in the 1840s, John Hood, wrote: "The more I see of

it and its neighbourhood, the more I am delighted with it: its fine ascents from the noblest harbour in the world; its bays, its coves, its gardens; . . . its forests of masts reflected on the glassy waters. . . . and the whole scenery around! I don't think the imagination of man can form a combination more pleasing." Another visitor of the same era described Pitt Street, Sydney's second most important thoroughfare, as "the Broadway and Oxford Street of the Antipodes" and was impressed by the "endless succession of well-equipped and lighted shops".

But this pleasant, bustling harbour city was soon rocked by a momentous event—the discovery, on February 12, 1851, of gold outside Bathurst, only 129 miles away. The lucky prospector was Edward Hargraves, who had left Sydney several years before to hunt for gold in California and returned without much wealth, but with the conviction that there was gold in Australia too. After a bit of initial prospecting, Hargraves was so certain of a strike that he reportedly put on a top hat and tails, to make sure he was suitably dressed for the occasion, chose a likely creek, duly panned some gold and announced to his young guide: "This is a memorable day in the history of New South Wales. I shall be a baronet, you will be knighted, and my old horse will be stuffed, put into a glass case and sent to the British Museum!" Hargraves' future was not so grand as his prophecy, but he was made a Commissioner for Lands in New South Wales, given a reward of £10,000 and a life pension, and presented to Queen Victoria in 1854.

Soon Sydney was the starting-point for a mad rush to the goldfields, which in the course of ten years yielded, in all of Australia, gold worth £124 million. Many of the city's residents closed their businesses or quit their jobs to join the rush. New speciality shops selling supplies for prospectors opened, as did gold-buying establishments that displayed in their windows "gold glittering in every variety and form" as well as "heaps of sovereigns and banknotes" to assure successful miners that they could be promptly reimbursed for the precious raw metal they found. The centre of activity soon shifted, however, for richer strikes were made near Melbourne in 1857, transforming that rather shabby town almost overnight into a thriving city. By 1860 its population surpassed that of Sydney—139,000 to 96,000—a lead it was to maintain until the turn of the century.

Although Sydney found its primacy upset by the growth of other cities during the gold rush, nonetheless it also benefited from the increased population and prosperity that gold brought. Many immigrants who came to look for gold gave up the idea and settled in the city instead, expanding the many services available in it. The new wealth from gold—and the continuing boom from wool—was also reflected in a building explosion. New, elaborately decorated, sandstone buildings quickly transformed Sydney into a Victorian city.

While monumental public architecture was the focus of interest, builders found profits could also be made by providing houses for the rapidly

Australian airforce veterans mass in Hyde Park, after their annual parade through the streets of Sydney in observation of Anzac Day on April 25. Originally held in remembrance of soldiers of the Australian and New Zealand Army Corps (Anzacs) who fell at Gallipoli in the First World War, the Anzac Day ceremonies also honour members of all fighting services who died in the Second World War, Korea and Vietnam.

growing population, which had reached 137,000 by 1871. Long rows of two-storey structures began to line the streets stretching out into what were then the city's outskirts—and are today its desirable inner suburbs. Large Victorian mansions rose along leafy streets in areas such as Hunter's Hill and Glebe, and some of these buildings remain among the city's most gracious residences.

In photographs from the 1870s onwards the moods of various parts of the city are captured: Hyde Park, where elegant ladies and gentlemen lounge on the grass for an outdoor band concert; the crowded commercial wharves with the masts of wool clippers rising like a leafless forest; beaches with children frolicking in the surf while adults stroll fully clothed along the shore; and forlorn buildings in run-down neighbourhoods, their walls covered with posters advertising Gilbey's Silverstream Schnapps, Bates' Dandelion Cocoa and Coffee, and Sander & Sons' Eucalypti Extract.

For an elegant evening out, there was the Marble Bar on Pitt Street, decorated with plaster and gilt, seven kinds of marble, brass, mirrors, paintings, carved woodwork and stained glass. In the 1970s, this bar was dismantled and painstakingly reassembled in the basement of a new height in luxury, the Hilton Hotel in Pitt Street. Other entertainments included the theatre (where Sarah Bernhardt appeared in 1891, while the *Sydney Morning Herald* rejoiced that other countries were finally becoming aware of the country's intellectual life) and the opera. The Australian

Museum moved to new premises in 1857 and opened its doors with, reportedly, a rather eccentric set of exhibits, including such curiosities as a bottle dredged up from the harbour with several oysters attached to its neck, one of which clenched a discarded tobacco pipe. An art gallery, begun in 1885, was opened with more conventional fare on display, and the Australian Academy of Arts organized its first exhibition in 1887.

However, progress was not apparent in all sections of the growing city. In some areas ladies pressed scented handkerchiefs to their noses to combat the odours rising from the primitive sewage system. There were other neighbourhoods ladies would never enter at all, where ramshackle tenement buildings leant against each other and dirty, ragged children played barefoot in the streets.

Numerous visitors to Sydney in the middle and late 19th Century re-marked that there was less crime than in London, but gangs of toughs, locally termed larrikins, hung about the city's street corners. They were easily recognizable by their style of dress: "a slouch hat worn on the back of the head . . . a bright handkerchief knotted round the neck, an overhanging shirt and very tight trousers". Some larrikins committed serious crimes— including murder. Others only made suggestive remarks to passers-by and "bashed down the hats of respectable citizens". Larrikins are now part of Sydney mythology—and many people will tell you they were forerunners of the hippies, staging a revolt against conventional society.

Both the splendours and evils of the Victorian age were in full blossom for celebrations of the city's centenary in 1888. Parades filled the streets, a regatta was held in the harbour and a balloon ascent took place from the Domain. Centennial Park was opened with fitting ceremony (and has since been saved twice from having a chunk taken out of it—in the 1890s as a site for a mausoleum for politicians, and in the 1970s for a sports complex), as was the new extension to the Town Hall. Numerous buildings were rushed to completion so that the significant date "1888" could be set above their doorways.

The stages of the city's development followed fast upon each other. An outbreak of bubonic plague in 1900 led to much-needed improvements in the sewage and water systems, and to extensive slum clearance. Federation of the six Australian colonies into the Commonwealth of Australia in 1901 came at a time when Sydney's streets were being widened and levelled, and much of the city was being electrified. By making it clear that Australia could not continue to rely on Britain for protection and prosperity, the two world wars spurred the growth of Sydney's industrial sector—and of Australia's budding sense of nationalism. The Depression of the 1930s brought new construction in the city to a standstill, but before and after the slump more and more suburbs were added, reflecting Sydney's prosperity and the general feeling that it is everyone's right to own a house and garden. Even so, in the mid-1950s architect Morton Herman could still proclaim Sydney to be a Victorian city, with here and there a towering structure of steel and glass, "somewhat like a gold tooth in a discoloured Victorian mouth". The 1960s and 1970s changed that. As skyscrapers multiplied, the 19th-Century structures seemed to shrink beneath them.

The memory of the city that I myself cherish most is from a point midway between the height of the Victorian era and the present. In 1938, I was nine years old when Sydney staged a major celebration to mark its, and Australia's, 150th anniversary. I shall never forget Garden Island (still a real island then, not yet connected to Potts Point by land reclamation), where life-size replicas of Governor Phillip's ships were anchored beside the grey warships of the Australian Navy. All over the city, shops and public buildings were hung with flags, and window displays were crowded with mannequins in 18th-Century costumes. Buildings dating from early times were picked out in lights, and trams and buses were gaily decorated.

On Australia Day, January 26, a procession marched through the city and an endless stream of floats wound beneath the window in Martin Place, where I watched with my family. No moment in Australian history was forgotten: here were the First Fleet, the convicts, the Rum Corps, gold rushers, explorers, settlers, soldiers—even famous racehorses had their place! These were the things that made us, that revealed the past to a nation awakening into self-consciousness—just as they did to the child I was then. This may have been the last time the country was to be offered to its inhabitants in innocence and candour; by the end of the Second World War, the city had experienced a coming of age: complexity and sophistica tion set in, and Sydney was transformed from the still-provincial city of my boyhood into today's bustling, international metropolis.

An Early Emphasis on Transport

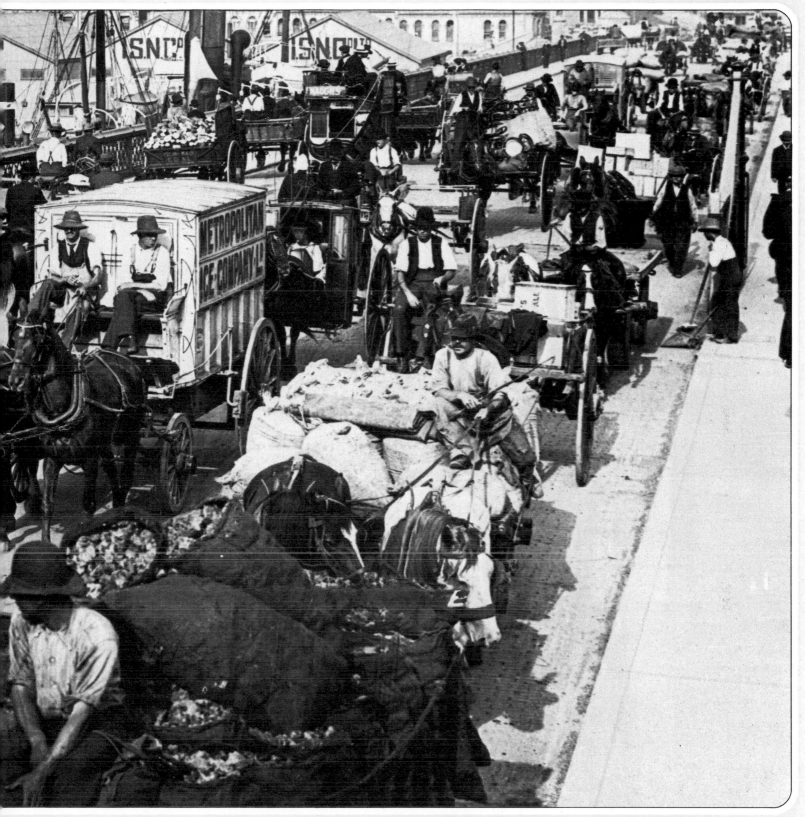

Peak-hour traffic in 1900 crowds the 42-year-old Pyrmont Bridge, a toll crossing for Darling Harbour. Rebuilt in 1902, the span is still a severe bottle-neck.

Since its earliest days, Sydney's urban sprawl along its complex coasts has posed problems of communication and commuting, and the city's changing solutions to its specific transport needs have made their successive contributions to the look of the streets. In the 19th Century, the few bridges crossing the creeks and inlets that divided the old city were often congested with horse-drawn traffic; steam ferries—some of them designed to carry vehicles too—formed the most direct links between many of the harbourside settlements. But like burgeoning cities all over the world, Sydney was transformed by the mechanization of transport. By 1900, railways and tram tracks joined the rapidly expanding suburbs to the city centre; and, as the 20th Century advanced, the motor car brought Sydneysiders a freedom of mobility that they have valued highly ever since.

In 1885, ranks of hansom cabs await customers in spacious Bridge Street, which today is overshadowed by the skyscrapers of Sydney's central business district.

On a rainy day in the 1930s, one of the last horse-drawn cabs to operate in Sydney evokes a bygone age of travel. Most such vehicles rapidly disappeared from the city's streets within a few years of the advent of the automobile.

A steam-powered "punt"—or square-ended barge—ferries a horse-drawn cart and several early motor cars across the Georges River from Tom Ugly's Point, 11 miles south of central Sydney. Today, traffic crosses here by the Georges River Bridge, built in 1929 as part of the Princes Highway that links Sydney with Melbourne, 440 miles away.

Day-trippers in the 1890s board a steamer at Manly Wharf for the cruise back to Sydney Cove, a seven-mile journey that now takes about 15 minutes by hydrofoil.

In the 1920s, Swan's Limited, an important Sydney hardware store, musters its modern fleet of delivery trucks, each emblazoned with its advertising slogan.

Local dignitaries board one of four new steam omnibuses in 1906 for a trial run in suburban Enmore. The buses proved unreliable and were withdrawn in 1907.

In 1901, the year of the federation of Australia, two ladies steal the limelight at Randwick Racecourse in a motor buggy, claimed to be the country's first.

A waiting steam tram offers passengers the
choice of riding on an open upper deck or on
a lower deck shaded by blinds. Comfortable but
smoky, steam trams replaced the horse-drawn
versions in 1879 but in turn gave way in
1905 to a system powered by electricity.

Sydneysiders scramble for places aboard an electric tramcar at King's Cross, on their way to the harbour to view the arrival in 1908 of the American fleet.

3

Unbinding the Ties to Britain

In a city where the majority of citizens are of British descent, it is no surprise that Sydney has many characteristics that would not be out of place in, say, London, or Edinburgh, or Belfast. It has its pubs and fish-and-chip shops, exclusive public schools and a bewigged judiciary. Sydney sportsmen play soccer and Rugby football and that most English of pastimes, cricket (although their conduct of the game is more robust than would normally be seen at Lord's Cricket Ground). Motorists drive on the left and, should they meet with a fatal accident, the odds are that they will receive a Church of England funeral, since the Anglican Church is numerically the principal religious denomination (followed closely by the Roman Catholic). And, of course, since Australia remains by choice a member of the British Commonwealth, Sydney's citizens owe allegiance to the British sovereign.

But one can no longer say—as one could a few decades ago—that Sydney is more British than any city outside the United Kingdom. As late as the 1950s, the citizens displayed a stubborn loyalty to British manners and mores that bordered on the masochistic, maintaining a self-discipline strikingly at odds with their climate and environment. At the height of Sydney's scorching summer, for example, office workers dressed themselves in heavy three-piece suits more appropriate to the City of London. Nobody dreamt of taking a siesta: like "mad dogs and Englishmen" they continued to go out in the fiercest midday sun. Christmas dinner —often digested when the temperature was more than 90°F—was the traditional feast of roast turkey, steaming plum pudding and piping-hot mince pies, although as a concession to the weather this Dickensian fare was often addressed alfresco, in the garden or on the beach. At the end of every performance in a theatre or cinema, the audience stood for the playing of "God Save the Queen", although the practice had already begun to fall into abeyance in England. Similarly, pubs were subject to restrictive licensing hours long since abandoned in "the old country"; most of them shut at 6 o'clock in the evening.

During my last visit to Sydney, I found that most of these customs were no longer in vogue. Pubs stayed open later in the evenings, salads and tropical fruits were being substituted for the traditional Christmas menu, and nowhere did I see a businessman wearing, as some did before the war, a black bowler. A certain decorum in dress was still observed, in places such as Martin Plaza and George Street, in downtown Sydney's commercial centre, but the typical businessman's garb was a far cry from the clothes of a generation before. Walking down Castlereagh and Elizabeth streets in

From a vantage point near the southern approach to the Harbour Bridge, a couple watch the annual Australia Day celebrations taking place below in Sydney Cove to mark the landing of the continent's first white settlers.

the morning rush hour, I saw plenty of office workers in formal shirts and ties; but most of them were without jackets, and many wore shorts.

The British national anthem is no longer the only song played at ceremonial events and state occasions. Now audiences also stand for "Advance Australia Fair". Attempts had been made since the early 19th Century to find Australia's own anthem, but no candidate had ever been officially selected. Then, in 1972, a contest was launched to find an original composition befitting "our national aspirations". The government offered a $14,850 prize to the winner, but none of the thousands of entries was judged worthy. In desperation, the government selected three indigenous Australian songs, from which the final choice was to be made by a limited public opinion poll. "Advance Australia Fair", the work of an immigrant Scottish carpenter published in the late 1870s, emerged the winner, and was adopted as the national tune—though not as a fully fledged anthem.

An important tie with "the old country" had already been severed in 1966, when the English sterling currency of pounds, shillings and pence was replaced by an Australian system of dollars and cents. The new dollar was worth 10 shillings of the old currency, or about one U.S. dollar. The then Prime Minister, Sir Robert Menzies, had strongly supported a proposal that the new basic unit of currency should be called a "royal"—an idea that met with massive opposition from people who thought the name was too suggestive of kowtowing to monarchist Britain. The proposal that the unit be called an "austral" had much wider appeal, but was rejected after somebody pointed out that Australians, with their penchant for running words together—especially for joining the "n" of the indefinite article on to the following word—would be sure to debase the currency by calling the new national dollar a "nostril".

Such changes, though hardly sweeping, were concrete evidence of the national consciousness that emerged after the Second World War. Ever since the foundation of Sydney, many Australians had supported separatism from Britain, but they were outnumbered by settlers who were dependent on the comfort of inclusion in the family of empire. With the decline of that empire, and the two world wars, Australia's strategic isolation in the south-east Pacific became more and more evident. Britain's military strength declined severely after the First World War, and the motherland could no longer be counted on to rush with armed forces to Australia's aid should the new country be invaded—as was feared—by Japan or China. That Australia must be prepared always to see to its own defences was made clear during the Second World War, when the imminent threat of Japanese invasion loomed very real indeed.

Gradually, with the boom in European immigration that followed the Second World War, Australia began to feel less "British" and, during the 1950s and 1960s, a thriving economy, a greater degree of self-sufficiency, and such technological advancements as television and cheaper, faster air

Preferring to slake their thirst outdoors on a hot summer day, young people in the suburb of Woollahra congregate outside a pub—usually still called a "hotel" in Australia because of a 19th-Century law forbidding the consumption of liquor except in residential premises.

travel all helped to reduce the population's sense of isolation. By the 1960s, a prospering Australia was sufficiently self-confident to begin the process of loosening its ties with Britain.

As British influences in Sydney have waned, the traditions of other ethnic groups have asserted themselves. Strolling through a shopping centre in Double Bay, with its sidewalk cafés and pastry shops, you could almost imagine you were in Vienna. In fact, the British hegemony in catering has been shattered generally by a proliferation of espresso bars, patisseries, delicatessens, pizza parlours, and restaurants that purvey every kind of European cuisine. The proprietors' names blazoned above these eating establishments suggest one explanation for the erosion of Anglo-Saxon traditions. Immigrants from Italy, Greece, Malta, various central European countries, Lebanon and China have contributed strong elements of the lifestyles of their homelands and have played an important part in creating a new ambience more in keeping with Sydney's equable climate.

The Italians are the largest European ethnic minority group in Sydney; about 200,000 live in the city, which has its own Italian newspaper, a plethora of Italian restaurants, and even a Dante society. Some parts of Sydney look as if they could have been transplanted from Italy. In Dural, for example, a suburb on Sydney's north-eastern outskirts, the houses lining the sunny streets always remind me of brick villas from some town in Tuscany. They may be a long way from Pistoia or Poggio a Caiano, but I find their architecture is recognizably Italian, and in them the owners can feel they have never totally dissociated themselves from the land of their ancestors. The centre of Italian life in Sydney is the old inner suburb of Leichhardt, three and a half miles south-west of Sydney Cove. Here, chemists' stores are likely to be labelled *Farmacia* and those of pastry-cooks are identified by a sign reading *Pasticceria*.

Sydney's Greeks, numbering about 130,000, are the next largest European ethnic group. In parts of Newton, Marrickville and other inner-city suburbs, the signs identifying the streets are printed in English but almost all others—those on shops and cinemas, for example—are in Greek. The customs of the homeland are evident everywhere in these neighbourhoods. In some sections of the city—and especially at Taylor Square in Darlinghurst—food shops offer every kind of Greek dish, from taramasalata to dolmades, providing exotic alternatives to Anglo-Saxon dishes.

Many of the Italians and Greeks who have made their homes in Sydney work in catering and related industries. A significant number of the inhabitants of Dural, for example, grow produce, and their harvests are handled and sold by their countrymen in Sydney's markets. Also, large Italian food-manufacturing companies have sprung up (one of them actually exports spaghetti to Italy).

But it would be a mistake to typecast any of the city's ethnic groups. The Italian or Greek or Yugoslav you see in national costume while celebrating a feast-day may just as well be a dentist or an architect or a journalist as a waiter or grocer. Italian immigrants, especially, have a reputation for industry, being willing to work long hours and to take on extra jobs in order to achieve higher living standards. Rags-to-riches stories in Sydney's Italian community are not uncommon. One well-known account of achievement concerns a fortune-seeker from Naples who arrived in Sydney in the mid-1950s. He began work as a low-paid builder's labourer but within a year had gone into business for himself. Two decades later, he had become the owner and managing director of an engineering firm with an annual turnover in excess of $20 million. There are countless similar stories and not only of material success. The immigrants have contributed a full share to the arts as well.

Although Sydney has grown increasingly cosmopolitan, any statement that the city is a true melting pot needs to be carefully qualified. It is not—and never has been—a multi-racial society. Some Australian advocates of republicanism, enthusiastically preaching on behalf of a complete political break with Britain, also exhort their countrymen to expunge all European sensibilities from their minds; yet, the fact is that Australia remains over-whelmingly oriented towards Europe—in its attitudes about everything, but especially race. As late as 1966, the official Australian strategy on immigration was devoted to maintaining a "predominantly homogeneous population". Since the policy had been formulated by European—mainly British—settlers, this meant that Africans and representatives of other non-European cultures were to be excluded from Australia.

The tool of this ideology—popularly called the "White Australia" policy—was the Immigration Act of 1901 that made all would-be immigrants subject, on arrival in Australia, to a 50-word dictation test, supervised by immigration officers, in *any* European language of the officials' choosing. Thus a brilliant Asian linguist could be rejected by being subjected to a test in, say, Dutch, although he was fluent in English and French and German.

At first, a very small number of ingenious candidates managed to exploit loopholes in the Act—discovering, for example, that if the test did not number exactly 50 words it was legally invalidated. But from 1909, when the rules were tightened, until 1958, when the test was finally abandoned, not a single non-white candidate passed the language examination. The scrapping of the dictation test signified merely an end to pretence. From 1958 onwards, the Minister of Immigration was empowered to refuse any application to enter the country without having to justify his decision. The door remained firmly closed to non-whites.

The "White Australia" policy was based on the usual, various factors; among them nationalism, prejudice, and fear of losing employment to immigrants who would do the same job for less money. But probably the most important element was Australia's special dread of the "Yellow

Peril"—the fear that the Japanese and Chinese would one day try to over-run the country in order to gain access to its rich resources or to acquire more living space. The "Yellow Peril" scare was at its peak between the two world wars, and only subsided when the long-standing bitterness, in-tensified by the Second World War, started to fade in the early 1960s.

The main wave of European immigration to Australia began in 1947, after the government, anxious about underpopulation and a low birthrate, had set up a special department to encourage settlers from the Continent as well as from Britain. European immigration continued steadily until the beginning of the 1970s, by which date non-British settlers accounted for more than half of the Europeans who had come to New South Wales.

But during the 1960s and 1970s the country's non-European popula-tion also increased dramatically; in the course of the 1960s the "White Australia" policy was gradually dropped by all the major political parties and, in 1972, a newly elected administration under Prime Minister Gough Whitlam instructed immigration officers to take a more positive and liberal attitude towards applicants from non-European countries. This trend towards liberalization was continued by the succeeding administration of Malcolm Fraser, which offered an amnesty in 1976 to visitors who had stayed longer than their permits allowed—irrespective of their countries of origin. All the 6,550 illegal immigrants who applied—almost half of them non-Europeans—were allowed to stay.

As a result of these changes, immigrants from countries in Asia and Africa increased in numbers from about 27,000 annually during the late 1960s to nearly 33,000 in the mid-1970s. Over the same span, the annual average from the U.K. decreased from 88,000 to 57,000—owing in part to the decision of the British and Australian governments to end a pro-gramme that had been inaugurated in 1947, enabling British citizens to sail to Australia at a cost to themselves of only £10 a head, or for nothing at all if they were ex-servicemen. (Though the so-called Assisted Passages Scheme continued, the fare payable by an immigrant from Britain approxi-mated to the actual cost of the journey.) Also, the number of applications from other European countries simultaneously began to decline.

In 1979, a policy was introduced whereby all those hoping to enter Australia—regardless of the country of their birth—were to be assessed on a points basis, and selected according to their skills, the demand for those skills, their educational standard, literacy, degree of fluency in English and their general attitudes. Even these restrictions were waived to accommo-date refugees fleeing from the war-torn countries of Indochina. Thus the already established upward trend of Asian immigration was boosted to such an extent that at the end of the 1970s it surpassed, for the first time, the numbers of any other racial group, approaching 30 per cent of entries.

Most of these groups, like the European ethnic communities, tend to congregate. The prosperous Chinese population is centred in the old

Wide-brimmed hats, worn by these visitors to the Royal Easter Show, instantly identify their wearers as out-of-towners on a visit to the city. Such adaptations of the traditional pioneer's bush-hat offer much-needed protection against the wind, dust and glaring sun of the outback.

market area, around Dickson and Hay streets near Darling Harbour. Though their dress is Western, as is their taste for cars and consumer durables, they adhere privately to traditional customs and ceremonies.

Food shops in the Dickson Street area sell dried fish, pressed duck and glazed chicken. Other merchants purvey all the supplies found in Chinese emporia the world over: delicate porcelain bowls and teapots, paper lanterns and mobiles, exotic tinned foods, bamboo furniture and fireworks.

But any new visitor to Sydney who entertains visions of exotic ethnic quarters that are isolated physically and psychologically from the rest of the city is in for a surprise; for whatever aspects of his native culture the immigrant may choose to preserve in his new home, and however much difficulty he may have with the English language, he regards himself almost from the moment of arrival as first and foremost an Australian.

Perhaps the characteristic of Australian life most prized by all its citizens is the deliberate stance of social egalitarianism. But the eager-to-please newcomer can find this self-conscious democracy somewhat confusing. Sydneysiders can be both reticent and garrulous, warm and argumentative —and it is difficult to predict which will be the more likely response at any given time. If you hail a taxi and get into the back seat, the driver may growl at you: "Is there something wrong with me, mate? Do I smell?" Yet, if you sit down beside him in the front seat and cheerfully engage him in conversation, you may be totally rebuffed. These days it is quite likely that the driver was born in, say, Zagreb or Naples, but that makes little difference; he will probably be even more determined to eschew class divisions and to behave as a free agent—to insist, that is, on his "Australianness".

The emphasis on egalitarianism, it seems to me, burns brighter in Sydney than in other Australian cities. Some sociologists account for it by looking to the city's past: it is their thesis that the descendants of settlers who survived in difficult conditions by their own efforts would prefer to be judged only by their achievements, and not by their wealth or their social credentials. A "good bloke", most Sydneysiders would agree, eschews pretensions. As one of them expressed it: "When I came here many years ago, I was warned not to put on too much 'side'. 'Go easy, mate,' they told me. 'Don't come the raw prawn.' In other words, don't be a snob, a prig, an arrogant, conceited, selfish or self-opinionated ass. People in Sydney," he went on, "take people strictly at face value. We don't have an elaborate social charade. Of course, we realize that everyone isn't truly equal, but we recognize that we all get along a lot better if we treat each other as though we were."

This attitude can be daunting to citizens from societies more reliant on rigid social divisions. In the late 1970s the well-known English journalist Peregrine Worsthorne visited Australia and was unsettled to discover that all three bars in the same hotel were crowded with a clientele that was "indistinguishable, with no visible gradations of rank or style". He went on to comment: "Perhaps this is as it should be. But it does not make for good

Sydneysiders make merry at a Christmas party aboard a cabin-cruiser as they head out into the harbour to watch the traditional Sydney-Hobart yacht race that starts every year on December 26. Christmas in Sydney coincides with peak midsummer temperatures, thus encouraging even Santa Claus to abandon the usual costume and equip himself with sun-glasses and a can of iced beer along with his cottonwool beard.

social theatre, so to speak, since everyone seems to be cast in the same minor role. The British class system at least forces people into different moulds, which produces a far more interesting social landscape than Australia's shapeless uniformity. And because everybody here is equal, and superficially at ease with his fellow, there is no need for manners or politeness, which are the gears required only in societies whose wheels do not all revolve at the same speed. So there is goodwill galore, unrestricted affability, but a total lack of grace and courtesy; without the tensions and frictions of a class hierarchy there is no call for such social lubricants."

Many will argue that the loss of "good social theatre" is a small price to pay for being rid of these "tensions and frictions" of the highly divisive English class system. But the impression of equality in Sydney society is, in some ways, superficial. One reason why class distinctions seem so blurred is the sameness of accent. In general, Australia does not have the wide variations of dialect that make regionalism so rich and varied a force in most other countries. Only a phonetics expert could tell from an Australian's speech whether he or she came from Sydney or Perth or Brisbane.

And within the confines of a single large city, variation is almost non-existent. A latter-day Professor Higgins could hardly walk up to a girl in the street (as his London counterpart did to Eliza Doolittle) and tell her that she lived in the improving part of Redfern, or that he could make her acceptable in Vaucluse after a dozen lessons in voice production.

There are, also, real drawbacks to the general commitment to egalitarianism. For fear of being labelled a boaster, a Sydneysider may deliberately underplay his strengths and achievements. Furthermore, the attitude has fostered a truculent streak. Many Australians regard the police as opponents. Similarly, they are quick to be suspicious of self-assertive leaders, whether they be in industry, politics, or even sport or the arts; they will seek to disparage them lest they get "too big for their boots". In the 1930s Jack Lang, Premier of New South Wales, won enormous popular support simply by promising his electors that he would "cut the heads off the tall poppies"—meaning people in high-earnings groups.

I am not suggesting that all Sydneysiders are social levellers; they are, as a group, stridently capitalistic as far as material success and its social importance are concerned. But they do insist that everyone is entitled to a "fair go". If one Sydneysider in a group launches into a sustained criticism of someone less voluble, almost certainly it will not be long before another cries out: "Hey, lay off, mate. Give him a fair go." If a boxer is annihilating his opponent in the ring, sooner or later some humanitarian will yell from the stands: "Give him a go." And similarly, if an immigrant should be struggling against an act of discrimination, eventually someone is likely to say: "Come on, sport. Give the New Aussie a go."

But there is one minority group of people that has not yet been accorded the "fair go" treatment: the descendants of the inhabitants who were already there when the first immigrants arrived. Dispossessed of their tribal lands and, in Tasmania, even hunted like animals by the early settlers, the Aborigines were exposed to, and stricken by, European diseases to which they had no resistance, and their population fell drastically throughout the 19th and 20th Centuries. They seemed a doomed race; but in the 1930s and 1940s, thanks largely to improved medical care, their population began to increase for the first time since white men landed at Sydney Cove.

In the 1960s Aborigines in Australia were belatedly accorded many rights previously denied to them. For the first time they could vote, own property and firearms, buy liquor, and qualify for unemployment benefits, free medical care and other social services. They were also entitled by law to equal pay with white workers—although, in practice, this requirement was often ignored. But fundamentally, the new government policy towards them was one of assimilation. Its purpose was defined at a conference of Commonwealth and state ministers held in Darwin in 1964: "The policy of assimilation means that all Aborigines and part-Aborigines will attain the same manner of living as other Australians and live as members of a single Australian community enjoying the same rights and privileges, accepting the same responsibilities, observing the same customs and influenced by the same beliefs, hopes and loyalties as other Australians." In short, it was intended that the Aborigines should cease to exist as a race apart.

Since then, Australia has adopted a more enlightened and humane approach. Aborigines have been included in official census totals since

Two smartly turned-out ladies converse in the Members' Bar at Sydney's Randwick Racecourse during the Spring Meeting—one of the premier annual events in Sydney's busy social calendar.

1967 and assimilation has been abandoned in favour of a policy that encourages them to maintain their own communities and preserve their own culture and traditions. But the change may have come too late. The old Aboriginal ways—characterized by harmony with the land, a lack of concern for personal property and the sharing of all possessions within the tribal group—are irreconcilably at odds with Australia's increasingly urbanized and materialistic society.

One of the most influential and outspoken Aborigines has been the poet Kath Walker, who brings to the expression of her people's plight a sympathetic directness and simplicity of emotion. As the first Aboriginal poet to be widely read and appreciated by white Australians, her success bears witness to their changing attitudes. One of her works expresses the bewilderment experienced by many Aborigines who find themselves living in cities; called "Municipal Gum", the poem is addressed to the native eucalyptus tree, transplanted to the city street where its roots are unnaturally surrounded by tar. "O fellow citizen," run the last lines, "What have they done to us?"

Though there are an estimated 60,000 Australian Aborigines still dwelling in the outback, they earn a meagre living mainly as stockmen and ranch-hands on cattle and sheep stations where they work for white employers; very few still lead a traditional nomadic life. The majority now live in cities, and in Sydney there are more than 20,000.

Of these, about 200 live in a separate community at La Perouse—an isolated, sandy area on the northern tip of Botany Bay. There they occupy dilapidated prefabricated housing, and most of them are without the skills or education that would enable them to compete for the rewards available in Sydney's competitive society. Elsewhere in the city, there are perhaps a hundred or so Aboriginal families who own their own homes and maintain an Australian suburban lifestyle.

The majority of Sydney's Aborigines, however, live in relative squalor in the inner suburb of Redfern, in a ghetto of terraced slum dwellings. It is possible to find as many as a dozen people sharing one small room. Many subsist on unemployment benefits. Alcoholism and malnutrition are major problems. It has been estimated that at any given time more than 20 per cent of the Aboriginal children in the city are suffering from malnutrition, and that 30 per cent of the community have diabetes, compared with a figure of 2 per cent for the overall population.

According to a doctor in Sydney's government-funded Aboriginal Medical Service, a large proportion of the Aborigines in Redfern live on only the cheapest and most easily available food, and never eat fresh fruit or vegetables at all. For many, the staple diet is white bread, white flour, white sugar, potatoes and tea; and the result of this excess of refined carbohydrates is that they suffer from a severe deficiency of vitamins and minerals. The same doctor went on to explain: "The thing that is stopping

Preserving the traditions of their original homeland, members of a Turkish-Australian community perform a folk-dance at a weekend barbecue in the suburb of Marrickville. The little girls are wearing the white-collared black tunics that are the uniform of Turkish primary schools. Large numbers of Yugoslavs, Greeks, Italians and Turks emigrated to Australia in the years following the Second World War.

Aborigines from eating better food is social repression. They are not motivated to want to feel better. The impact of white civilization has left them confused and without pride or sense of dignity. How to restore that dignity and pride remains an eternal problem."

For the most part, white Sydneysiders have been blind to how the Aborigines ("Abos") have been existing, but in recent years their awareness has been intensified. With increasing knowledge has come greater concern, and Redfern is now the centre for a variety of organizations devoted to bettering the Aborigines' condition. The Medical Service has been running for several years; more recently legal aid and lobby groups have been set up by the Aborigines themselves.

One hopeful sign of a return of "dignity and pride" was the opening in 1974 of the National Black Theatre, with the help of a government grant, in a converted factory in Redfern. There the language, dance and mime of the Aboriginal lifestyle were revived, and young urban Aborigines—who had never actually lived in the bush—could learn about the traditions and rituals of their ancestors, recovering some of the cultural identity they had lost in the course of the last 200 years.

Every city has its stereotypes and Sydney is no exception. Until a few decades ago, the typical Aussie male, as depicted by many writers, was a rugged individualist—tall, keen-eyed, hatchet-jawed, laconic and relaxed —a European toughened and made self-reliant by his pioneering background. It was an image sustained overseas by Australia's exemplary fighting men in two world wars and reinforced by a procession of disciplined and fiercely competitive Aussies who made their mark in international sport.

More recently, a much less flattering stereotype came to the fore. This modern Aussie—whose image has been popularized by Australian satirical writers and television character-impressionists—is pot-bellied and loud-mouthed. His interests are entirely limited to beer, sex and sport. He regards women ("sheilas") as a necessary comfort, sees the cultural arts as pursuits suitable only for homosexuals ("poofters"), talks through his teeth with a nasal accent and uses his fists to settle the frequent pub arguments he gets into.

This caricature is worthy of attention because the manner in which it has evolved and gained prominence reveals much about Australians in general, and about Sydneysiders in particular. Australians have always acknowledged that there is in their midst a large number of brash, beer-swilling, chauvinistic and uncultured characters labelled "Alfs". For a long time, the "Alf" was a familiar character in Sydney. However, during the new era of Australian nationalism that emerged during the 1960s and 1970s, this vulgar type was superseded by the "ocker", a colloquial name of uncertain origin that may have derived from the term "a knocker"—meaning someone who is forever criticizing things. This stereotype was given substance

At a Roman Catholic procession on All Saints' Day in west Sydney's Five Dock district, Australians of Italian descent carry a statue of St. Anthony of Padua, adorned with lilies and supporting a figure of the crowned infant Jesus. Sydney is predominantly a Protestant city, but since the 1950s the proportion of Catholics has risen to more than 25 per cent, as the result of immigration from Catholic countries in Europe.

An oil refinery tank adorned with brightly painted images of Australian life looms over Italian family burial vaults in a cemetery at Yarra Bay in south Sydney.

by a fictional character called Ocker, played by the actor Ron Frazer in a television series of the late 1960s. It was the beginning of a nationwide craze whereby the ocker—originally a crude, self-satisfied male chauvinist —was elevated by the media into a kind of national symbol.

Initially, many different versions of the character emerged. Anyone blatantly, impenitently Australian—especially if excessive and uncouth—is called an ocker; and, whether used approvingly or accusingly, the term fits the native of Sydney fairly well. It is ockerish to be loud and truculent, but also to be respectful of courage, physical or moral. At his crudest and simplest the ocker was portrayed by satirists as an oafish, bare-chested sports spectator, shouting vulgar abuse at the umpires and non-Australian players. He would have a schooner (15-fluid-ounce glass) of beer in his fist, thongs (rubber sandals) on his feet and a beer-belly bulging out of his tee-shirt and spilling over his shorts. Alternatively, he might be depicted as a muscle-bound athlete doing press-ups on Bondi Beach, now and then pausing to make a lascivious remark to a bikini-clad "sheila" passing by.

Another version was invented by the Australian satirist Barry Humphries in the 1970s. Humphries introduced to the public a character called Les Patterson, a politician who, having been appointed to a government post in London, describes himself as "Cultural Attaché to the Court of St. James". Patterson, as played by Humphries, presents a bottle-red complexion, a beer-belly and tombstone-size teeth. Convinced that culture is a racket, he is nonetheless willing to serve the new Australian nationalism and bring some authentic Aussie culture to Britain—though in ghastly taste intended to outrage all civilized feeling. As he puts it: "I thought I'd give them an Abo show. Sober up a few Abos, put them on a Cathay Pacific inaugural [an airline flight; Humphries is always excruciatingly specific about details] and hire a London theatre." The revolting Les is invariably drunk, but always assures his audience: "I'm not full." He tends to end each sketch by confessing that he *is* drunk really: "I'm full as a Catholic school"—a phrase that both captures Australian idiom and refers to the traditional antipathy between Catholics and Protestants that exists in Australia as elsewhere.

Humphries' caricature took firm hold on the nation's imagination, but a more realistic personification was Paul Hogan, a blond, blue-eyed compère who first appeared on Australian television in the mid-1970s. Hogan—a maintenance rigger on the Sydney Harbour Bridge—entered a television talent contest as a result of a bet with his mates: quite unrehearsed, he talked in front of the cameras about any subject put to him, and enchanted his audience with witty iconoclastic remarks delivered in an authentic Sydney vernacular. He was an overnight success: handsome enough to be a film star, but nevertheless a rough and typically warm-hearted Sydneysider, devoid of pretensions, a man's man, fond of his booze, knowledgeable about sport and, above all, pleased and proud to be Australian. The fact that he talked in local clichés and was scornful of anything beyond the boundaries of Sydney added to his appeal; and soon his face was appearing all over the city on hundreds of posters advertising a brand of cigarette. He had become the quintessential "good ocker".

In the Australian advertising world it then became unfashionable to use well-spoken characters to promote goods on radio and television. Instead, there was a demand for colourful ockers who might appeal more effectively to the common man. One successful choice was a builder's labourer who was used in the mid-1970s to advertise a new Sydney shopping centre. On television, he was shown standing high up in the cradle of his crane, lauding the new shops below in the unadulterated vernacular and nasal accents of a true-blue ocker. The man undoubtedly had charisma. Unfortunately, success in this new field persuaded him that he might have a future as a real actor, and so he paid for elocution lessons. It turned out that no one wanted a builder's labourer who talked like Prince Charles and his hoped-for film career never got off the ground.

The country's love affair with ockerism was for a spell extraordinary. Eventually, of course, Australians became heartily sick of the craze. Nevertheless, the type has clearly earned a permanent place in the national mythology; and there is indeed a bit of the ocker in many Sydneysiders. Millionaires and beachcombers alike, with ocker-style assertiveness, will tell you that Sydney is the greatest city on earth, with the best beaches, best wild life, best climate and best standard of living. If challenged to defend his claims, the ocker may go on to say that Europe is class-ridden and full of snobs. Proud of the peaceful history of his own country, he will claim that the culture of the Europeans is a poor recompense for the wars they have generated. He is, above all, an isolationist, but he is knowledgeable about the rest of the world; he may know the strength of the current in the Zaire River and can probably tell you the form of government in Andorra.

This kind of pundit—the Sydney "expert"—who can be found in any Sydney pub most nights of the week, reminds me of how Gertrude Stein described Ezra Pound. "He was a village explainer," she said. "Excellent if you were a village, but if you were not, not." Sometimes, I think Sydney is the biggest village in the world.

Carnival at Eastertime

The daily Grand Parade of prize-winning livestock creates circular patterns in the 5½-acre main area of the Royal Easter Show's multi-pavilioned complex.

Every spring, more than a million people crowd into Sydney's Moore Park for the traditional 10-day Royal Easter Show, the supreme agricultural fair of a country that has more than 1.75 million square miles of rich grazing land devoted to sheep and cattle raising. Nowadays, however, less than one-tenth of Australia's work-force is engaged in rural occupations and the retreat from the countryside is reflected in the changed character of the Sydney show. In addition to livestock-judging and other bucolic events, it now presents within its 70-acre showground a programme that includes rodeo and circus acts, polo, hot-air balloon races, precision parachuting, motor cycle stunt riding, jazz bands and carousels. Palpably, the colossal show—first held in Sydney in 1869—has developed into one of the most diverting carnivals in the Southern Hemisphere.

In the tent-pegging competition, a galloping contestant uses a steel-tipped lance to pick up a wooden peg embedded horizontally in the turf. The skill was first developed by tribesmen in India to uproot tents during surprise attacks on encamped caravans and was adopted as a sport by the British cavalry in the 19th Century; in Australia it is now practised mainly by the mounted police. Four-man teams compete by making a succession of peg-spearing runs: four abreast, singly and in pairs. The team collecting the most pegs is the winner.

In the first leg of a wine-waiters' race to publicize Australian wines, competitors weave among obstacles towards the bottles they must uncork and pour out.

A contestant in the second leg returns smoothly with champagne-filled glasses.

In a contest of speed and skill, a professional woodcutter—identified among those competing simultaneously by a numbered card, shown edge-on at the top of the log—follows his own roughly chalked guidelines as he chops away. A top performer can sever a 15-inch log in less than 50 seconds. Axemanship has been mostly superseded in Australia's 94 million acres of commercial forests by use of the powered chainsaw, but the craft is kept alive as a sport by professionals who tour the country to compete for prize money in local shows.

Pressed against the outer frame by centrifugal force, visitors ride one of the funfair's dizzying attractions.

A team prepares for a contest between four hot-air balloons that will remain tethered to trucks. The first balloonist to rise to the hundred-foot limit wins.

In the main arena at Moore Park, four drivers aboard sulkies contend in the show's trotting programme. Trotting races have been enormously popular in Sydney since the 1940s, when restrictions on betting at floodlit evening meetings were removed; at Harold Park alone, the city's main trotting track—one of six in the metropolitan area—racegoers place bets totalling $120 million annually.

4

The Currents of Prosperity

Sydney's dynamism derives not only from its geography and history but also from its life as a centre of national—and, indeed, international—economic and political importance. It is the senior city of a country that enjoys an advanced capitalist economy and all the characteristics of affluence to be found in the developed countries of Europe. Australia also offers marked contrast to even the most highly developed of its geographical neighbours in the Orient, by virtue of the vast living space it can afford its small population, its self-sufficiency in food, and the enormous potential wealth of its mineral resources. In spite of the worldwide economic pressures that built up during the 1970s, Sydney boasts one of the highest standards of living in the world.

The city, of course, owes much of its good fortune to its coastal assets. Its extensive port functions as the channel for the wealth, mainly agricultural, of its hinterland. Yet, to passengers arriving by sea, the bustling cargo docks that give evidence of the city's commercial might are surprisingly unobtrusive, tucked away west of the Harbour Bridge in the bays and inlets of Darling Harbour and Pyrmont. More than 250,000 passengers arrive by boat each year—some 90,000 of them on vacation cruises, the rest travelling for business or pleasure from domestic and foreign ports. But most of them alight at Circular Quay, while the majority of cargo vessels and container ships sail on beneath the bridge (built with a 172-foot clearance to allow lofty commercial vessels to pass beneath it) and empty their holds somewhere along the harbour's 10 miles of industrial wharfage. The building of a mammoth new container terminal at neighbouring Botany Bay, begun in the early 1970s, brings within range Sydney's current goal: the doubling of cargo capacity so that its docks can handle some 35 million tons of goods annually.

Sydney is one of the largest wool ports in the world (it was exporting more than 1.3 million bales of wool a year at the end of the 1970s) thanks to the enormous flocks of sheep raised on the grasslands beyond the Blue Mountains. The wheat grown in the same region is a second major export; many farmers allocate part of their land for wheat and graze sheep on the remainder, rotating the uses in successive years.

Manufactured goods, timber, coal and uranium are also exported through Sydney's docks. The last of these, mined primarily in Australia's Northern Territory a thousand miles away and exported for use in nuclear industries, brought protest marchers to Sydney's dockyards during the 1970s. The numbers of the demonstrators were swelled by those with a

A 50-storey office building soars above a futuristic sculpture on Australia Square in Sydney's central business district. The 560-foot-high circular tower, part of a complex that occupies almost a whole city block, was built in response to rising land values and a demand for prestigious downtown office space.

related—and wholly Australian—cause at heart: the valuable uranium is extracted from land to which the Aborigines attach age-old religious significance, and the exploitation threatened to disturb their sacred places.

In the past, most of the cargo arriving in Sydney was warehoused along the docks, to be prepared for trans-shipment; but now the container ships farrow their neatly packaged litters on the dockside, and articulated lorries move them along to consumer goods stores and wholesale distributors in many parts of the country. Containerization was introduced in a big way in the late 1960s and, within a decade, more than half of all goods passing through Sydney's docks had been encased in clean, efficient modules. But the process has transformed the mood as well as the technology of the dockyards. Modern commerce seems bent on keeping the docks as neat as a graduate business school; the container ports are never dirty and untidy, as the old docks were—merely bleak.

I remember the time when the tall brick warehouses fringing the waterfronts of Darling Harbour and Pyrmont were alive with activity. Rising above them were the spars and derricks of merchant vessels from every part of the world; the emblems and pennants flying from them always reminded me of the pages in school atlases that illustrated the flags of the world and the national maritime insignia. Now, with the need for warehousing reduced, a number of these lofty, many-floored structures are deserted. There is, however, still something romantic about their scale and confidence; they speak of a bygone era of low ground rents and fortunes made in trade by merchant adventurers and entrepreneurs with secrets sometimes as dark as their black frock-coats.

In spite of the drop in harbourside employment that accompanied containerization—offset to some extent by the hirings for the new Botany Bay terminal—Sydney's industrial dockland still employs many hundreds of workers in a variety of occupations such as stevedoring, shipbuilding and repair. The modern docks, no less than those of the pre-war period, have their fascination; for this noisy mechanized world is as much a part of Sydney's soul as the surfing beaches and quiet creeks. It is a fascination that I have felt ever since the days when, as a child, I used to stay with my grandmother in Woolwich. One of my uncles would set up a telescope on the wide veranda facing directly across the harbour to Balmain on the south shore. I would be invited to tell the time from the face of the clock on Balmain Town Hall. Dutifully I reported the time and then quickly trained the telescope on the enthralling cranes and slipways of the dockyards.

The name of Woolloomooloo Bay, located almost a mile east of Circular Quay, has amused generations of visitors by its mere sound—although pronouncing it seems as natural to Sydneysiders as saying "Manhattan" does to New Yorkers. Sydneysiders agree the word is of Aboriginal derivation, but no one seems to know exactly what it means. It may come from *wullaoomullah* meaning "young kangaroo", because

Prospective buyers inspect bales of wool in a cavernous warehouse at the Sydney Wool Centre, opened in 1975 in the western suburb of Yannora. Handling the grading, selling and dispatch of up to 700,000 bales of wool a year, the Centre is the principal market-place for the world's biggest wool-producing country.

these animals once thrived in the area, or from an Aboriginal word for the windmills that, in the 19th Century, lined the hill above the bay: *wooloon* meaning "whirling" and *mullah* being derived from an Aboriginal rendering of the English word "mill". In any case, the docks along the eastern shore of Woolloomooloo Bay served for more than a century chiefly as a cargo port. In 1956 berths for ocean liners were added, and in the 1970s various ambitious schemes were proposed for developing the entire waterfront area as a passenger terminal complete with hotels and shops, to function, alongside Circular Quay, as a worthy approach to the city.

From the edge of the same bay extends a promontory named Garden Island—a double contradiction of its present nature; for it is covered with giant cranes and screeching machinery instead of flowers, and it is surrounded by water on three sides only. Once it was a true island, separated from the peninsula of Potts Point by a channel of water 330 yards wide; but it was connected to the mainland in the 1940s as part of a reclamation project to provide emergency dry docks for British warships in the Pacific. It is now the site of the Captain Cook Graving Dock—one of the world's largest centres for ship repairs.

Two miles west of the dominating Sydney Harbour Bridge lies Cockatoo Island, the harbour's largest island and the site of two smaller graving docks as well as an extensive shipbuilding yard. Every inch of space on it now seems to be devoted to maritime fixing and building, but the island was once covered by eucalyptus trees—the roosts for countless white-plumed cockatoos. Between the arcadian past and the mechanized present, in the days when Sydney was a penal settlement, Cockatoo Island served as a punishment centre for difficult convicts. After 1840—when transportation of British felons to Sydney ceased—until 1908, the island continued to serve as a prison.

As a matter of fact, during the city's convict days, several of the harbour islands now put to maritime use served as dreaded punishment yards. One of them was Goat Island, situated a bit more than a mile east of Cockatoo Island and named, it is thought, because goats imported by the First Fleet settlers were put to graze there. It has a shipyard, too; and also located there are the headquarters of the port's fire brigade and of the dredging and wharf-maintenance service. But Sydneysiders well versed in the darker side of their city's history may think of Goat Island in terms of a convict named Charles Anderson, who was transported to Sydney in 1834 for smashing shop windows in England during a drunken brawl.

Confined with other prisoners on Goat Island, Anderson made repeated escapes that were punished with appalling severity. He was eventually sentenced for two years to the unusually cruel punishment of being fastened by a long chain to a rock in the open. Passers-by in boats took pity on him and tossed him bits of food. Finally a deputation of human-itarian settlers approached the Governor to have him removed before his

Banks of criss-crossing escalators link three floors of the huge Roselands shopping centre in the south-western suburb of the same name. The growing decentralization of industry has made it possible for increasing numbers of Sydneysiders to adopt a self-contained suburban lifestyle, and has encouraged a demand for regional shopping centres that offer a range of goods and services comparable to those to be found in the great stores of the inner city.

sentence was over. Anderson was sent to work in a lime kiln; escaped and lived with the Aborigines; was recaptured and finally came under the care of a remarkably liberal and compassionate warden devoted to the cause of prison reform. The convict, still only 24 years of age, was sympathetically rehabilitated by being given responsibility for a team of draught bullocks that he gradually learnt to care for. Though he remained a prisoner, his behaviour improved so much thereafter that he was eventually put in charge of a harbour signal station. Nevertheless, perhaps unsurprisingly after his ordeals, he ended his life insane. Amid the commercial bustle of modern Sydney Harbour the legend of this much-punished Prisoner of Goat Island casts another revealing sidelight on Sydney's history.

The city's main commercial wharfs are located just south of Goat Island. Darling Harbour—one of the largest depots on the coast—lying immediately west of the bridge, exports meat. Nearby Glebe Island—again, not really an island but a peninsula attached to the mainland—is the site of a major wheat terminal, where giant silos can, by means of chutes, unload their grain on to waiting ships at a rate of 1,700 tons an hour. Some 1.5 million tons of Australian wheat are exported annually from Glebe. Across a small bay at Balmain, another sophisticated conveyor system at the Number 1 berth loads coal at a rate of a thousand tons an hour. Almost all of the three million tons of coal exported from Sydney each year are shipped from here.

There are gigantic coal seams, broken up by outcrops of shale, lying 3,000 feet below Sydney itself. The seams curve upward, coming near the surface in a crescent around Sydney. There are, altogether, more than 80 mines along them, capable of producing about 50 million tons of high-grade coal annually—75 per cent of Australia's output. Coal is mined from the seams 80 miles to the north, in the Hunter Valley, and exported from Newcastle (named after the renowned British coal city); 40 miles south at Wollongong; and 60 miles west at Lithgow. Both Newcastle and Wollongong have iron-and-steel industries as well as coal mines. Among them, Sydney and its brawny twin industrial neighbours claim three-quarters of the population of New South Wales and thus wield tremendous influence not only economically but also politically. Indeed, some Australians hold that N.S.W. ought to stand for Newcastle-Sydney-Wollongong.

The docks are an important contributor to Sydney's prosperity, but they are not the city's only commercial face. In the 1930s, the urban population had passed the one-million mark and the growing work-force—both manufacturing and clerical—provided ample evidence that Sydney was already a much more complex economic organism than a mere staging post for exports. Today, the skyscrapered commercial centre stretches two miles behind Circular Quay, testifying to Sydney's position as Australia's leading centre of white-collar employment.

Sydney first entered the skyscraper era in the 1960s; until 1957 there was a strictly enforced height limit of 150 feet—approximately 12 floors—for both office and residential buildings. But Sydney's cramped business district, confined by the water of Darling Harbour to the west and by an extensive park to the east, had to expand somehow. The first structure to take advantage of new concessions in the height regulations was the Australian Mutual Provident Society's 26-storey head office at Circular Quay which was opened in 1962. The building met with considerable opposition from people who liked the scale of Sydney the way it was. But, despite the protests, the A.M.P. building was soon followed by numerous others nearly as tall, and several even taller. By the late 1960s the skyline was dotted with cranes as the designs constantly rose higher. Confronted with the question Sydneysiders love to ask—"What do you think of our city?"—visitors were tempted to take a studied look around and reply with the old line: "Should be quite nice if you ever get it finished."

Now that the commercial centre at Circular Quay has been transformed into a world of glass towers, many Sydneysiders find they quite like it. Architects, keeping in mind that Sydney's climate is considerably warmer than New York's and that Sydneysiders are outdoor people, have provided numerous pedestrian plazas and open spaces to give an airy look to the tightly packed, narrow streets. At lunch-time, the plazas are full of office workers eating sandwiches, reading novels and enjoying the sunshine and the sea breezes that waft in from the harbour just down the street.

The beehive activity in the business district is in large measure owed to the discoveries, beginning in the 1960s, of large deposits of valuable minerals. The continent is now believed to have the world's largest reserves of three important minerals: bauxite, rutile and zircon. The first yields aluminium; the second, the light-weight metal titanium; and the third is used in alloys and paints. Australia also has the second largest deposits of uranium and lead, and the third largest reserves of silver, zinc and iron ore, as well as substantial deposits of phosphates, nickel, tin, gold, oil and, of course, coal. These discoveries provided the lift for the economic buoyancy of the 1960s and early 1970s—when mineral exports quintupled in six years.

At the time, the boom must have come as a surprise to some Australians. There had been an embargo on the export of iron since 1938, after a government report had warned that, if known reserves were not conserved, the country would, in little more than a generation, need to import ore for its iron-and-steel industry.

But the pre-war Australian government also had a political motive for banning exports and its intentions were conveniently supported by the report on iron resources. Fears about the territorial and economic ambitions of Japan had always been an influence on Australian foreign policy and this anxiety increased in the years just before the Second World War. The government was eager to put an end to investment in the production of Australian iron by the Japanese, who might use it to make arms.

The export ban served the purpose of limiting the Japanese role without political offence; but it also meant that, with exports prohibited, companies had little incentive to look for new deposits. After the end of the war, the embargo remained in force, since it was still against Australia's interests to assist the Japanese economy.

The export ban was finally lifted in 1961. By this time, memories of the hostilities of the Second World War had dimmed and relations were more friendly. Japan had become a highly industrialized nation, in need of raw materials but with few resources of its own—a perfect Pacific market for Australia's mineral wealth. More importantly, perhaps, the balance of power in South-East Asia had changed substantially and Japan was badly needed by the West as an ally against the spread of Communist regimes in Asia. Once the ban was lifted, in the course of the great minerals rush of the 1960s, the country discovered 50 times more iron than was known to exist when the original gloomy report was presented in 1938.

Another reason for the rapid succession of finds was the enthusiasm with which Australians greeted the discoveries. It only cost a few dollars for a prospector to stake a claim if he thought he had discovered valuable mineral deposits. Prospectors who had previously searched for gold and found instead other unexpected and unidentified substances went back to re-examine them; some of these finds turned out to be uranium or nickel.

With the new awareness, some Australians literally stumbled into wealth. A stockman on a cattle station in north-western Australia told this story of

West of the city centre, ships of many nations lie berthed at the piers of Pyrmont (foreground) and alongside the waterfront of Darling Harbour (background).

Warehouses, goods yards and factories sprawl over the 10-square-mile area of the city's commercial dockland. The containerization of cargo (right) was introduced in the 1960s, and by the mid-1970s accounted for more than half the freight handled in Sydney's docks.

his rich copper finds: "I was out with my two sons rounding up cattle when the big bay I was riding stumbled and fell. I was there rubbing my leg when I picked up a rock. I thought to myself, 'Strewth, that's heavy.' And no wonder. The flaming thing was all copper."

While most of the mineral discoveries occurred far from Sydney, in the interior of the continent and in Western Australia, wealth from them immediately flowed into the city. They had a particularly strong impact on the Sydney Stock Exchange. The smaller Melbourne Exchange remained more staid, but in Sydney everyone wanted part of the action. In the late 1960s and early 1970s the floor of the Stock Exchange was packed with off-duty taxi-drivers, students, housewives, businessmen and secretaries. The over-enthusiasm meant that a company's stocks climbed wildly at the slightest rumour of a find—and fell just as rapidly if it proved false.

The scramble on the Sydney Exchange lasted several years, but slowly quieted as amateur investors realized they could lose money as quickly as they could make it. Discoveries began to come less frequently and the effect of the general recession of the mid-1970s also had its influence.

Opportunely, the expansion of minerals production came at a time when the country's foremost chief export was under pressure; the rapid increase in the popularity of synthetics during the 1950s and 1960s meant that the demand from textile manufacturers for wool fell off sharply. In the early 1950s—when agricultural products (including wool) made up 80 per cent of the country's exports—Australians had boasted that their country "rode on the sheep's back"; but by the end of the 1970s agricultural products made up slightly less than half of all exports. During the same period minerals rose from 5 per cent of exports to more than 35 per cent— with just one mineral, coal, earning as much as wool. In fact, Australians involved in the wool business realized with some relief that the long-term threat from synthetics was not as bad as it initially seemed and, in view of the soaring price of oil, from which so many synthetics are made, indications are that in future natural fibres will not only retain, but possibly increase, their share of the market.

But the move into a more diversified economy has raised complicated issues that Sydneysiders and other Australians debate continuously. To some, exporting vast amounts of the nation's substantial, but finite, mineral reserves seems like "selling part of the farm": it provides money for the present generations, but what about those to come?

Further, some chauvinists see their country being reduced to the status of "Japan's quarry"—with Australia's raw materials serving as the source of Japan's industrial might, rather than their own; they therefore espouse development of home industries that can process various ores in Australia, thereby increasing profits and providing new jobs.

Many Australians are deeply concerned about depending too heavily on the Japanese market. Japan has become Australia's largest customer,

Weighing-in at more than three-quarters of a ton, a prize Hereford bull—tagged with its entry number, birthdate and weight in kilograms—receives a critical appraisal in the judging ring at the annual Royal Easter Show. By the late 1970s, Australia was the world's greatest exporter of beef: 50,000 cattle a week were being slaughtered in the abattoirs of Sydney alone, and the city's ports handled more than 1.5 million kilograms of beef and veal a year.

absorbing more than 30 per cent of all Australian exports. This reliance developed partly as a result of Britain's entry into the European Economic Community in 1973, with the effect that the U.K. had to buy more from Europe and less from Australia. Britain's share of Australia's exports had fallen from 30 per cent in 1950 to less than 5 per cent by the late 1970s.

Investment within the country by foreigners has proved to be another hot issue. In sparsely populated Australia, funds are always needed to develop the mineral finds. But Australians question how much money should come from abroad; how much control foreigners should have over the minerals; and what share of the profits should go into foreign pockets.

With more than 300,000 factory workers, Sydney is the largest manufacturing centre in the country. Firms have been attracted not only by the city's port facilities, but by its population of more than three million, which provides the largest work-force and the largest consumer market in Australia.

The factories are concentrated in several parts of the city. The old inner suburbs, such as Balmain and Pyrmont, have small factories and workshops interspersed among the houses, whose residents are accustomed to living with the background rumble of machinery producing clothes, leather items, furniture and a variety of other goods. The outer suburbs, to the west and south of the city—besides harbouring older, post-war factories—have attracted modern industrial development, such as electronics, food processing and pharmaceuticals. Many of the newer buildings are neat and functional and feature a flowing lawn and a manicured garden out front. Driving by, it is often impossible to tell what functions they fulfil, unless a discreet sign gives the secret away.

Heavy industries are situated west of the city centre, along the upper Parramatta River—the waters of which now suffer from serious industrial pollution. I have sometimes suspected that there must be a rule of nomenclature whereby the more romantic a district's name is, the more unpleasant will be the reality. Thus, moving west along the Parramatta, the suburb of Concord harbours gasworks; Auburn has abattoirs; and Silverwater petrochemical plants. Elsewhere are railway workshops, engineering works and factories producing agricultural machinery.

An even greater concentration of factories is to be found near the shores of Botany Bay. Here, too, is Kingsford-Smith Airport, named after Sir Charles Kingsford-Smith, a pioneer Australian aviator who was one of the founders in 1930 of a service that provided flights between major cities in Australia. Most Sydneysiders refer to the airport as Mascot Airport, after the suburb in which it is located.

The visitor arriving by air descends through a haze of industrial pollution to touch down on a runway that extends into the somewhat murky waters of the bay. More than 1.5 million overseas passengers and almost five million domestic travellers pass through the airport each year. Until the fine bypass of the Southern Cross Drive was opened in 1969 the most direct route from the airport to the heart of the city was a five-mile drive through district after district of factories, repositories, breweries and slum neighbourhoods. The scene is so grim that visiting dignitaries were sometimes even re-routed a longer way round in order to provide them with a better first impression of the city.

Botany Bay began its industrial life early; its first manufacturing plant was ex-convict Simeon Lord's factory, opened in 1815 to produce woollen cloth and blankets. The area's isolation from the main settlement at Sydney Cove and the ease with which waste could be dumped into the bay also attracted "noxious trades" such as tanning, glue and soap making, and wool scouring. Wool was—and still is—brought to Botany Bay to be cleansed of impurities, and combed to separate out the long wool fibres; the adjective "Botany" has since become synonymous worldwide with wool of very fine quality.

However, it was not until the First World War that Australian manufacturing industry really expanded. Before the war Australia had relied on Great Britain for most of its manufactured goods. Because of the disruption in production and communications caused by the hostilities, the flow of commodities dried up and prices rose. With the forces of supply and demand thus unleashed, Australia was producing more than 400 new kinds of manufactured goods by the time the fighting ended. During the Second World War domestic industrial growth made another spurt and Australia became a major supplier for the Allies' Pacific front. Many of

Botany Bay's industries, including food processing plants, chemical laboratories and paper mills, trace their origin to this period.

Botany Bay's most visible industry is one of its newest: a petroleum refining complex, opened in 1956, that ranks as one of Australia's two largest. From the air, the harbour is lit by tongues of red flames from chimneys burning off excess gases.

No modern industrial civilization would be complete, of course, without an automobile-manufacturing capacity. Sydney has its plant at Botany Bay for the production of General Motors' Australian car, a model called the Holden. The G.M. plant, located in the Botany suburb of Pagewood, assembles more than 35,000 vehicles a year. The Holden, which first came off the production line in 1948, was the first car designed and built in Australia for Australians and, for a time in the 1950s, held half of the domestic market; by the late 1970s it had slipped to 28 per cent, as the result of competition from imports, particularly those from Japan.

It is only fitting that Sydney should be the centre for automobile manufacture since the city is the most car-persecuted conurbation I have ever encountered. When I'm in Sydney I feel that there is an apocalypse threatening the city—a tidal wave of cars that will overwhelm the place and its inhabitants alike. Many families have two cars, some even four; in Sydney's centre there is virtually nowhere to park them and, with the city's traffic jams growing ever thicker, it may be that soon there will be nowhere to drive them. The State Pollution Control Commission has warned that photochemical smog in Sydney, produced in part by vehicle exhaust, is verging on the high levels already reached in Los Angeles and Tokyo. Also, the attractive, undulating and twisting streets, the indented harbour shore, the spacious suburbs are usually disfigured by lines of parked cars.

Sydney's traffic problem is largely a result of the city's inadequate public transport system and is made worse by the huge extent of the suburban sprawl. True, there is an extensive metropolitan bus service; but Sydney has only two underground railway lines, one serving the downtown area and the other connecting the eastern suburbs with Circular Quay. The suburban railway system has had only minor additions since the turn of the century—and most of the 160,000 Sydneysiders who commute by rail daily would like to see a great deal of improvement. Since lines radiate outwards from the heart of the city to the distant suburbs, a resident of one of the western suburbs who works outside the centre has almost no choice but to drive to work.

Naturally the presence of the harbour and its extensive network of waterways complicates the city's traffic problems. The two bridges that span the harbour, the Gladesville Bridge to the west and the Sydney Harbour Bridge, between them carry more than 230,000 vehicles each day. The Sydney Harbour Bridge—a "symphony in steel", as it was imaginatively described during its construction—was completed during the Depression of the early 1930s. Planned in better times—the prosperous and confident early 1920s—the bridge was intended to be a symbol of prosperity; as it happened, its progress served to keep people's minds off their Depression-related problems. The two halves of the bridge met in September 1930, to the click of a multitude of cameras; and since that event it has been impossible to think of Sydney without the image of this masterpiece of engineering.

Nonetheless, all through the stages of planning and construction, the Sydney Harbour Bridge (called, in those early days, the North Shore Bridge) became the focus of much political drama and conflict. When legislation to authorize the building of the bridge was debated in Parliament in 1922, a member of the Country Party, which served the interests of wealthier graziers and farmers, proclaimed: "I say it is a wrong thing to build the city railway and the North Shore Bridge when we need railways in the outback." Nevertheless, the city interests prevailed and the bridge was built. On the day of the opening, however, a different political conflict hit the headlines, when a right-wing extremist stole the left-wing Labor Premier's limelight by charging into the ceremony and cutting the ribbon before the Premier was able to do so officially.

The bridge's association with flamboyant political gestures serves as a reminder that the political process has made an important contribution to the excitement and vigour that characterize Sydney—even if the city's political activities are much less obvious to the tourist than its commercial muscle. Sydney is, of course, the state capital of New South Wales and was well established long before there was a federal government of Australia; the state Parliament holds extensive powers, since the governmental responsibilities in Australia are divided between the national and state levels. The national government, which meets in Canberra, has an upper and lower house on the British pattern. Its responsibilities are listed in the Constitution and include defence, foreign policy, welfare, immigration, and currency policies. All powers not specifically assigned to the federal government are left to the states—including education, internal transportation and health; but in the post-war years the federal government has begun to play an important role in these areas too. Ideally, the state and national governments should work side by side, with neither dominating the other. In fact, however, during the last decade the federal government has continued to increase in power, so that the rights of individual states have become an important issue that is debated more and more in Sydney and throughout Australia.

At the city level, a curious and complex state of affairs exists. Sydney is divided into 41 municipalities, each with its own council, responsible for such areas as sanitation, road repairs and zoning regulations; and although in certain areas of legislation the councils' activities are co-ordinated by a

Ferries ply across the harbour in 1930 beneath the unfinished sections of the Sydney Harbour Bridge. Its completion in 1932 reduced ferry traffic by half.

Bridging the Gap

During the worldwide economic depression that followed the Wall Street crash of 1929, the people of Sydney watched a slow-motion drama unfold in silhouette against the sky: the building of the 1,650-foot-long Sydney Harbour Bridge, then the greatest single-span bridge anywhere in the world. Although some critics considered the $20 million cost unjustifiably extravagant, the steel structure was described by others as an "iron lung" that helped breathe life into the city by creating jobs for thousands of unemployed workers. Now recognized as one of Sydney's greatest assets, the 160-foot-wide bridge takes about $5 million in tolls from the 56 million or so vehicles that cross it every year.

Before a huge crowd of onlookers, a gala parade celebrates the inauguration of the Sydney Harbour Bridge on March 19, 1932. Presiding over the ceremony was Jack Lang, the Labor Premier of New South Wales, but before he was able to cut the traditional blue ribbon, a right-wing army officer, Captain Francis de Groot, charged forward on horseback and did the job for him with a swipe of his sword. De Groot—snapped in a smudgy photo at his moment of triumph (inset) was arrested and fined for "using threatening words, and cutting a government ribbon". The ribbon was re-tied and then, with a pair of jewelled scissors, Lang solemnly severed it, declaring the marvellous bridge open.

single authority called the Department of Local Government, there is no single body responsible for the city as a whole. Much of the day-to-day business of the state government is in fact concerned primarily with the metropolitan area; it is the state, and not the local councils, that has control of the city's police force and transport system, for instance. Various other boards and authorities have been set up with responsibility for water, electricity, major roads and some aspects of health and welfare.

The state government meets in Parliament House—an elegant, two-storey colonial building on Macquarie Street, featuring wide verandas and graceful columns—which is one of the two remaining wings of the colony's first general hospital. Built in the early 19th Century during the tenure of Governor Lachlan Macquarie, the hospital was known to Sydney-siders as the Rum Hospital because the Governor, short of cash, paid for it by allotting jointly to its three contractors a three-year monopoly on the lucrative rum trade. The central portion of the original Rum Hospital was torn down in the 1890s to make way for what is today Sydney Hospital, still an antiquated and inconvenient Victorian building. The south wing was converted in 1853 to house the colony's Mint and is still known as the Old Mint Building although it is now used for state government offices.

Other buildings scattered around the city have been acquired or built to house the expanding state administration; they include one 38-storey structure with darkly tinted windows located in the city centre, which is the headquarters for the state government's administrative departments and is known to Sydneysiders as "the Black Stump".

Although Sydneysiders unconcerned with matters of government might like to ignore politics altogether and concentrate instead on sun and surf, such apathy is against the law in Australia. Since 1924 voting has been mandatory in all state and federal elections; and in 1978 the requirement was extended to cover municipal elections as well, with fines for failure to cast a ballot. The average citizen therefore goes to the polls as often as once a year, since officials must be chosen both for the national and state Parliaments, and for the municipal councils. Popular referenda are also held periodically on important issues or on proposed amendments to the Constitution.

Most Australians vote for one of the two major political parties: the Liberal Party, which follows conservative politics emphasizing free enterprise and individual initiative, and which is supported by the business and financial communities; and the Australian Labor Party, which stresses social welfare and is supported by the trade unions—an especially strong and well-organized force in the industrial complex of Sydney, Newcastle and Wollongong. There is a third major constituency, represented by the National Country Party, which is in more or less permanent coalition with the Liberal Party. It speaks for rural interests and thus gets few votes in Sydney itself, though it usually holds a number of seats in both

A plain-clothes bodyguard (left) tackles a protestor demonstrating against the Vietnam War in front of Lyndon Johnson's limousine during the U.S. President's visit to Sydney in 1966. The direct involvement of Australian troops in Vietnam, beginning in 1965, generated increasing dissent from 1966 onwards, when selective drafting was introduced. Not since the massive demonstrations against conscription towards the end of the First World War had Australians been so actively critical of their country's role on the international stage.

national and state Parliaments. Several smaller parties have also been active in the city, including left-wing groups, such as the Communist Party of Australia and the several splinter groups that have broken off from it, and the Democratic Labor Party, a right-wing faction dominated by Roman Catholic members.

Australians are traditionally conservative in temperament: they had had only nine Labor Prime Ministers out of a total of 23 by the end of the 1970s. Yet, during the 1960s and 1970s, protest marches became a popular form of political expression as an "alternative" means of voicing opinions. The first issue to take a large number of Sydneysiders on to the streets was the Vietnam War, and the government policy of drafting young Australians to serve in it. The demonstrations against the war began to gather strength in the mid-1960s and reached their peak in December 1970 when 30,000 protesters took part in a so-called Moratorium March and sit-in at the Sydney Town Hall.

Opinion polls showed that opposition to Australian involvement in the war spanned both major parties. Certainly the students, trade unionists, and men and women of all political affiliations who paraded through the streets and clashed with police and officialdom over the issue of the war lost a certain political innocence that had previously characterized Australian life. The street politics ushered in by the Vietnam War were adopted for a number of other causes, including women's rights, environmental issues, gay liberation and Aborigines' land claims.

The protests against the Vietnam War were an indication of the growing change of mood in Australian politics that culminated in the election of a Labor government in 1972—the first break in conservative rule in more than 20 years. During the campaign, Gough Whitlam, the leader of the Labor Party, took a stand against the use of Australian troops in Vietnam and one of his first acts as Prime Minister was to end the drafting of Australian men to serve in the war in southern Asia.

Sydney had traditionally been the Australian Labor Party's base; and Whitlam—an eminent lawyer who represented the suburb of Cabramatta, an industrialized district on the city's western edge—inherited a whole constellation of urban problems awaiting solution. But the overall thrust of the Whitlam regime was the development of a new national consciousness that would take the country beyond being Britain's stepchild or a second cousin of the U.S.; it was his desire to create a new Australian identity that captured the spirit of the times.

This Labor government was in power only for a brief three years and its demise in 1975 long remained a topic of heated political debate. That year was an exciting one in Sydney and political passions ran high as it became clear that a massive confrontation between the Labor government and the Liberal opposition was brewing. Whitlam had stuck to his campaign promises of increased spending on education, especially at the university level, and he initiated endowments to the arts, contributing significantly to a blossoming of Australian culture. Millions of dollars were committed to badly needed urban projects and new directions— such as overtures to mainland China—were set in foreign relations.

However, in 1974 the Prime Minister was in trouble. He had tried to centralize the federal government by bypassing the states on some projects and working directly with municipal councils. This move alienated most of the state premiers, always touchy on the subject of their rights against federal interference. Further, the economy was in difficulty, in part as a result of the worldwide recession, but also, some argued, because Whitlam was more interested in social welfare and foreign policy than sound domestic economics, and simply let things get out of control.

By May 1974, Whitlam's legislation was being blocked by the upper house, where Labor's voting power was exactly matched by a coalition of the Liberal and Country parties. (In Australia, when there is a tie vote, a bill is considered defeated.) When, in June 1975, a Labor senator died, and his state premier replaced him with a Whitlam foe, complete stalemate had been reached. The upper house found it had the power to stop the passage of supply bills by which the government got its funds. The Australian federal government began, quite simply, to run out of money.

Through the first 10 days of November, Sydneysiders thought and

A Sydneysider conspicuously clad in a red shawl emphatically expounds his views at "Speaker's Corner" in the Domain, a 125-acre public park of open grassland adjacent to the city centre. For more than a century the Domain has served as the city's most popular venue for mass meetings, demonstrations and public debates.

talked of little other than the mounting crisis. Then, on November 11, it was resolved in a way that amazed the public. Sir John Kerr, whom Whitlam himself had recommended to the appointment of Governor-General of Australia (the British monarch's representative who, everyone thought, had only ceremonial duties), stepped in and dismissed Whitlam from office, asking Malcolm Fraser, the Liberal Party leader, to form a caretaker government.

Whitlam's astonishing ejection was followed by a national election on December 13, 1975, which the Liberal Party won by a landslide victory, proving that Kerr had not misjudged the sentiments then current among Australians; the majority of them clearly wanted a return to the stability of the conservative days. But many of Kerr's fellow countrymen, including scholars of constitutional law, have continued to discuss the legal basis and future implications of this action.

Seeing the Queen's representative suddenly take on so much power focused some of the vaguely republican sentiments that exist among some Sydneysiders and increased the popularity of the Republican Movement, an *ad hoc* group that spans several political parties and aims at the establishment of the Republic of Australia and the repudiation of all links with the British monarch. They are also against excessive foreign investment in Australia.

During 1975 I was living in the old inner-city suburb of Balmain, an industrial stronghold of both the Labor Party and the Republican Movement. Balmain's residents are made up mainly of two groups: the families of men who have worked on the nearby docks all their lives or in the area's numerous small industries, and fashionable newcomers, who want to live near the heart of the city and so have bought houses in Balmain, renovated them, and then set about trying to push the noisy industries out of the neighbourhood. Both groups are mainly Labor Party supporters, but the ambitious newcomers often have little in common with the factory and dock workers, with the result that local Labor Party meetings in Balmain are often lively affairs—sometimes even to the point of fisticuffs—for instance when planning-and-development strategies are discussed.

When I came to live in Balmain, I found it an atmospheric and stimulating place to be. There were, in the mid-1970s, several versions of subversive home-made republican flags flying in Balmain streets. Most had a white cross on a blue background with stars in each corner: the insignia of the goldminers who, in 1854, staged a rebellion at a settlement named Eureka, 60 miles from Melbourne. They were objecting to what they considered unfair licensing fees and regulations; about 150 miners built a stockade which they defended against forces sent in by the Governor. The fighting lasted less than an hour, but 29 men—24 miners and five soldiers —were dead when the shooting stopped. Eureka quickly became an Australian legend; Karl Marx saw in the episode the beginning of a workers' revolutionary movement in the country and one Australian politician went so far as to declare: "Australian democracy was born at Eureka."

One of the best ways to sample the issues that are on people's minds is by taking a Sunday afternoon walk through the Domain, the 125-acre park just east of the central business district that has become the forum for informal political debate among Sydneysiders. The park's soap-box orators draw huge crowds and, while the speakers include extremists of every persuasion, some of the men and women who attract the largest audiences are not cranks but individuals who are deeply concerned about the future of their city and country.

In 1964, the Sydney journalist Donald Horne addressed his complaints about the direction Australia was taking to the nation at large by writing a book of social criticism which he entitled *The Lucky Country*—no doubt with irony intended. But the phrase was so apt that Australians picked it up and began to refer to their land in all seriousness as "the lucky country". Whenever I walk through the Domain, I find I must agree with the masses: Australia is a lucky country and Sydney, a lucky city—lucky to have the lively discussions that take place in the Domain, to be able to boast of one of the best-paid work-forces in the world who enjoy one of the highest standards of living, to be endowed with mineral riches, to be in the midst of a cultural and intellectual awakening, and to have gained the self-confidence to explore new directions in its relations with other countries.

A dozen years later Horne wrote a sequel to his earlier book, called *Death of the Lucky Country*, in which he lamented the demise of all that was hopeful and lively in the Australia that had flourished in the early 1970s. His criticism was stimulating and his "shock therapy" seems to have been welcomed by his fellow countrymen. But his second title is surely in error. Sydney is there to prove it—a city intellectually, politically and commercially very much alive, boisterously and vigorously determined to make the most of its happy circumstance.

A Juxtaposition of Styles

A statue of Sydney's founder, Arthur Phillip, adorns the Lands Department Building of 1890—dwarfed by Farmers and Graziers House, completed in 1972.

Two building booms a century apart helped to reshape the face of Sydney. After the discovery of gold beyond the Blue Mountains in 1851, much of the riches that flowed into the city's economy was translated into massive public and commercial buildings. These handsome structures in the Victorian style gave the city centre a distinctive atmosphere: solid, ponderous, respectable. The 1960s brought a second mining bonanza from the search for base metals, such as nickel and iron ore. While foreign investment in such explorations brought the city new status as a thriving financial centre, the architectural emphasis was changing. Glass and concrete skyscrapers reared rectilinear shapes above the old skyline of turrets and spires. The side-by-side contrasts that appear everywhere contribute to Sydney's characteristic zest and variety.

A corner of the 610-foot-long Queen Victoria Building, designed in 1893 to rehouse the city's old open markets, abuts on the National Mutual Building of 1977.

Resembling the rungs of a giant ladder, the 64 storeys of the Mutual Life Centre, completed in 1978, rear over a former public house, now glowing with red paint.

A web of steel cables—part of the revolutionary design of the Centre Point Tower of 1980—stretches above turn-of-the-century commercial buildings.

Offices of the Electric Power Transmission company, built in 1976, flaunt the puzzling geometry of their windows above a conventional drab factory building.

The ornate pillars of the Bank of New South Wales in Pitt Street, built in 1893, adjoin the sleek façade of the Imperial Arcade shopping centre, erected in 1965.

A grandiose pediment high on the roof of the Lands Department Building is overshadowed by the headquarters of Colonial Sugar Refining, finished in 1966.

5

Nature's Pervasive Presence

The judgment is widely held that Australians have been moulded by the haunting emptiness of their huge country. (In the outback, it is true, Australians speak of how many acres there are to the sheep, not how many sheep there are to the acre.) And, the logic of the shibboleth proceeds, all that space is psychologically terrifying; there is so much land that it is easy to hate the very sight of the ever-unfolding terrain; thus, Australians have become among the most urbanized people on earth—with two-thirds of the population living in the six largest coastal cities. Sydney, specifically, is considered the embodiment of the all-or-nothing option allegedly facing every Australian; in the well-known catch-phrase—coined early in colonial history and still popular—it is "Sydney or the bush!"

Most of Australia's population is indeed gathered into its cities. However, even in Sydney—the continent's oldest established urban settlement —an awareness of the special topography of the land, penetrated as it is by some of the most complex harbour and river channels in the world, is constant. The uncompromising presence of nature actually infiltrates the city to its innermost fastnesses—to waterfront gardens, to small cleared areas by industrial sites, and to municipal parks forever bent on reverting to wildness and extravagance.

All over Sydney among the trees, shrubs and plants introduced by the settlers—remnants of the ancient bush still survive to remind Sydneysiders of the untamed world they have struggled to supplant. For one thing, there is plenty of room for nature within the city, whose population of some 670 people to the square mile can be compared, for example, with London's 11,500. As a result, given Sydney's sprawl and its occupants' enduring aspirations to home-and-garden ownership, the open space that in most great cities is organized into large central public parks is, instead, parcelled out into hundreds of thousands of private gardens.

In addition, in many outlying suburbs the houses seem to straggle out into the bush itself. And the area administered by the city is virtually ringed by two million acres of national parks, where the primeval bush is preserved from development. Further inland lie the precipitous ravines and wooded slopes of the Blue Mountains. Alone among the world's great cities Sydney flourishes within the omnipresence of nature.

Throughout the city the old and fearful world of the bush comes awake when the sun sets. I know of no city so eerie to walk in after midnight. Once, at about 3 o'clock in the morning, I took a taxi ride from the south side of the harbour to Lindfield on the north shore and, as we wound our

Hovering over outlying homes in the south Sydney suburb of Engadine, a helicopter tracks a bush-fire on the fringes of the Royal National Park, a 58-square-mile reserve of bushland. Many fires, sparked by lightning, fallen power lines, human carelessness and other causes, break out every summer in tindery bush areas near the city, but with calm weather conditions, as in this case, they can usually be rapidly contained by volunteer bush fire-fighting teams.

way along the Lane Cove riverside between the suburbs, both my driver and I tried to account for the strange sensation we were experiencing together: some sort of ungovernable, ancient and imperial presence. The driver was a practical, down-to-earth man and I am a sceptic; but the feeling was palpable to both of us, reminding us that the aura of the place —whatever its source—is immeasurably older than the earliest European who died on the same soil.

To the Aborigines there was nothing sinister about their ancient and rugged homeland, with which they felt inalienably identified. Their rich mythology told of an era in the far-distant past known as the "Dreamtime", when their sacred forebears, the Dreamtime people, had wandered the earth and given the land its present shape and character. Certain physical features of the landscape—rock formations, water-holes and the like— were created and given form by the spirits of the Dreamtime people; and, as the Aborigines travelled their nomadic life over the intimately known land, they followed in the footsteps of their ancestors. In this symbiotic relationship, the Aborigines found and left the land largely undisturbed.

But, if the Aborigines seem to have moved contentedly above the surface of the country, the white colonists trod doubly hard on it. The history of Sydney—as of Australia—has been one of battling against the sternly resistant terrain; for most of the settlers, the often infertile and very unfamiliar landscape of the bush projected deep animosity towards all those who were trying to make it their home. Rather than learn to live in relaxed proximity to their habitat in all its unwelcoming aspects, they were

In the exclusive north shore suburb of Killara, an architect's home is stepped into the slope of a wooded sandstone outcrop, gaining shade and seclusion among the blackbutt, turpentine and pittosporum trees. Sydney architects increasingly seek to integrate private dwellings with natural surroundings, so as to develop rugged terrain without disturbing the distinctive character of the Australian landscape.

intent on showing the country they were its masters. Even today, although conservationists and ecologists argue persuasively for the preservation of what is left of the natural scene, the majority of Australians still prefer a hard-nosed, commercial approach to their recalcitrant world—and nature, in turn, takes its revenge.

Right in the heart of Sydney, the reprisals can take on very concrete forms. I once heard a talk on BBC radio about the perils of ordinary life in Sydney that imparted something of the sense of besieging nature that I myself feel when I am there. The speaker was Clive James, a Sydney journalist who, in 1962, brought his considerable talents to London, where he wrote for several British newspapers. In the broadcast, James deliberately exaggerated in order to delight his comfortable British audience; but his point was legitimate. To the usual city dangers of cars and smog, he claimed, Sydney adds more unpredictable menaces: there can be floods, hurricanes, drought and bush-fire, to say nothing of the smaller difficulties of poisonous snakes and spiders, unpleasantly spiky bushes and plants, and unfriendly sharks. As James put it, the sharks are likely to "swim down your bathroom taps"; black snakes cruise along the north shore's Pacific Highway looking for a lift; and red-back spiders (a variant of the American black widow spider) are "forever staging uprisings in your lavatory".

Sydney also boasts a spider species, the funnel-web, that is even more venomous than the red-back; indeed, the male is said to be the deadliest spider in the world. The funnel-web is so-called because of the distinctive funnel-shaped cobweb that this large, dark-bodied creature with shiny black legs weaves at the entrance to its burrow. There is no known antidote to its poison, but fortunately it will leave you alone unless you attack it.

Not long ago a friend of mine had an ultra-modern glass and aluminium extension added to her house in the Lane Cove area. To make way for it, the builders had to dig up a venerable clump of dwarf palms in the garden, beside which the family had sat, unconcernedly, for years. They found in the roots a vast colony of funnel-webs. My friend was told that this was no unprecedented incident: colonies of them are frequently found even in the asphalt and concrete city centre, especially when old buildings are demolished for redevelopment. Every year many Sydneysiders are bitten by spiders of one kind or another, and among the old and sick such bites sometimes even result in death.

Every country has a predominant colour or tone. England's is a luxuriant green; the United States is vast enough to accommodate many shades, with the sumptuous orange and brown tones of New England in the fall complementing the desert hues of the Rockies and the rich primaries of California; and so on. But Australia, bleached by the insistent sun, is dominated by a sparse and pinched set of colours, unlike those of any other place I have seen. Australia's unique flora and fauna, evolved during aeons of isolation, have of course been infiltrated for nearly two centuries since the first European settlers introduced plants, animals and birds from the rest of the world; yet, even close to Sydney, the bush retains its unmistakable character, providing a peculiarly light, spacious and shadowless impression.

Australia's predominant tone is fawny-yellow, shading towards olive-green and blue, with lusher tones in areas where water runs freely. Native trees do not carry the heavy foliage of the European deciduous varieties, but keep their leaves throughout the year. On the other hand, many of them shed their bark constantly in straggling shreds. In addition, since the temperature swing between summer and winter is relatively slight—from an average of 57°F in July to 72°F in January—the look of the bush changes little during the year.

The leaves of many kinds of eucalyptus—Australia has an estimated 500 species of this indigenous family—hang straight down, receiving the sunlight on both sides, and the underside of the leaves may be any one of a dozen shades of silver. The native grass is more stalk than leaf. The yellow flowers of the multiple wattles (acacias) are loose and fluffy, while their leaves are at once dusty and sparkling—like those of olive trees. The tea trees, so-called because the settlers tried to make an infusion of their leaves as a substitute for tea, have abundant white flowers, and the rugged banksias—shrubs named after Cook's companion, Joseph Banks, who first collected them—carry flower-spikes of every hue, from scarlet through yellow and orange to green.

The gum trees (another name for eucalypts) and the native bushes tend to grow far apart, revealing the bark-strewn ground beneath them. Erosion has further exposed the surface of the soil and left many sandstone rock faces and escarpments on which even the hardiest plants cannot take root. In a characteristic Sydney valley or creek gorge, hundreds of boulders are exposed—like pieces of some antique fortification, or dolmens of an earlier civilization.

The palette of Sydney's colours is linked also, of course, to the city's climate. If you look out from a vantage point on one of the suburban hills at 7 o'clock of a summer's morning, with the promise ahead of a scorching day, the feeling is electric; this early, the prevailing sense is that of freshness, a promise of great liveliness. Viewed at midday, there is a heat haze and, in the torpor of that hour, the city appears to languish in its own air. Always, the sky is a conniving partner to the changes. Usually it is a blank and thoughtless blue, but when it is clouded over, that is a sign of real disturbance; the summer rain that makes the eastern coastal strip of Australia so fertile and habitable, compared with the rest of the continent, often falls very suddenly, in short, tropical storms and deluges.

The glorious, habitual sunshine does not necessarily contribute happiness. Weeks of unabating sun can produce a feeling of depression or

A variety of indigenous Australian plants, often extremely difficult to cultivate, flourish in a rocky corner of a horticulturist's prize-winning garden (above) near Mount Kuring-gai in north Sydney. The bright red flower in the background is the waratah, adopted as New South Wales's floral emblem (shown in detail, right).

pointlessness. The sun blazes down on Sydney's hedonistic surfers, but it also dries the creeks and water-holes, and turns the carefully cherished lawns of proud suburban householders to dusty acreage. All through the long summer days, the water-sprinklers play upon the grass and gardens of the wealthier homes on Sydney's north shore. Beyond these Eden patches, however, the hills and surrounding plains burn to a yellow evenness, and the atmosphere is hazy with high-floating smoke from the numerous fires consuming the bushland to the west of the city, in the Blue Mountains and beyond.

In this hot climate, the undergrowth dries out very quickly after rain, and bush-fires are one of the hazards that Sydneysiders are always aware of, even in the heart of the city. I remember a year when, after a spectacularly hot season, the fires invaded the gardens, parks and villas of Katoomba and Blackheath, some 70 miles away in the mountains, and the resulting pall of smoke drifting above Sydney itself suggested the aftermath of a bombing raid. People went into their backyards to find littered there, perfectly intact, carbonized leaves; they had been whipped up by the convection currents of the burning shrubland and been carried high in the air to drop—baneful visiting-cards hinting at the worst of intentions—on the city.

During the period of highest danger between October and March—and especially when there has been little or no rain preceding the hottest summer months, from December to February—bush-fires pose a constant threat to Sydney's outlying suburbs. Lightning is the major known natural cause of the conflagrations, but an estimated 50 per cent of them are the result of human carelessness: a cigarette tossed into the undergrowth perhaps, or a camp-fire insufficiently doused or allowed to get out of control. In rural areas ill-planned "burning-off" operations—the deliberate clearance of brushwood, by fire—is another major cause. Once started, the bush-fires burn fiercely—sometimes for weeks on end—fuelled not only by the undergrowth but by the oil that is secreted from the eucalypts' leaves.

Bush-fires, their prevention and extinguishing, are the subject of extensive efforts at control. In some conditions, the danger in the high-risk period may reach such proportions that the local governments will put an embargo on the lighting of any kind of open-air fire in specified areas; and all Australians living on the edge of the bush are versed in the techniques for survival, should they or their homes be threatened.

A friend of mine was once trapped by a fire that cut the road both to the front and rear of his path as he was driving down a four-lane freeway south of Sydney. He steeled himself to obey one of the cardinal rules for survival —not to leave the car and try to outrun the fire—and remained crouched on the floor with the windows wound up. He tried to summon the confidence to believe the survival manual's assurance that doing this while the flames pass gives the best possible protection against heat radiation—by far the most common cause of bush-fire deaths. Although the heat of a bush-fire is intense, it does not last long: the flames only take a few minutes to burn off the brittle undergrowth and dry grass, and therefore usually pass much too quickly to set a car alight. The front of the fire rushed towards him very fast, like some wild animal, and jumped the road in an explosive swirl of smoke and crackling flame. Both my friend and his car survived the ordeal. But he admitted to being very, very frightened.

The pioneer spirit of those who confronted the emptiness of the outback lives on, you might say, in the Sydney suburbanites who devote long hours to bringing order and beauty to previously wild tracts of land that seem never to have come under the care of any loving hand. Ever since my childhood in Brisbane, when I watched my father labouring happily for hours in the one and a half acres surrounding our suburban house, I have been convinced that a garden is a potent symbol of human love and contentment. No city has done more to strengthen my conviction than Sydney.

Among the local gardening enthusiasts there are uncompromising purists who insist they will admit nothing to their care that is not native. Indigenous gardens had a particular vogue during the 1970s, when for a time the *Sydney Morning Herald* included a class especially for them in its annual gardening competition.

Some of the rarer native shrubs successfully tamed by Sydney gardeners can indeed be as beautiful as they are delicate. I have seen some with leaves so tiny that they give the branches the appearance of slimly outlined exhalations of blue smoke. But the purist has great problems to contend with: the native plants seldom oblige him with an enthusiastic response. Evolved over centuries to suit exactly their particular niche in an unchanging environment, their root systems—able to withstand long periods of drought—cannot survive when transplanted to soil that is artificially enriched and cared for. Some of the more beautiful varieties of wattle, banksia and eucalypt stubbornly refuse to prosper in urban plots. The spectacular crimson-flowered waratah, floral emblem of New South Wales, can also be recalcitrant. And there are fine-leaved, delicate-bloomed wild flowers that adorn splendidly the low shrub bushland around Sydney; but uproot them and bed them down in suburbia and they too will die, however lovingly attended. They reserve their sweetness for their native heath.

Sydney's more practical suburban botanists mix imported shrubs and flowers with the more amenable of the indigenous species, such as the lemon bottle-brush, a tall shrub that grows best in well-watered soil. In doing so they follow no less an example than that set by the Royal Botanic Gardens, 70 acres of central Sydney that Mrs. Elizabeth Macquarie, the Governor's wife, helped to lay out at the beginning of the 19th Century. Many of Australia's wild plants were first domesticated here, but the gardens also contain one of Australia's largest collections of non-indigenous plants.

Bathed in tree-filtered sunlight, a row-boat glides over calm waters in Lane Cove National Park, a four-mile-long stretch of countryside preserved in the midst of Sydney's vast urban sprawl. The river banks support mature native trees such as eucalypts and angophoras of many varieties, including a Sydney red gum (foreground), whose sap readily bleeds from lesions made by insects or breaking branches.

Sydney's temperate climate, combined with the variety of its soils— sands, loams and clays—permits plants to grow all the year round. In consequence many kinds of vegetation from Europe, the Americas and the Orient can make themselves at home here.

The result is that the typical Sydney garden is as ecumenical as a council-of-churches assembly. By the low, wooden front fence, fringed with border plants, there are a couple of banana trees fruiting beside a palm tree, and—soaring a hundred feet above a privet hedge and the cement drive to the garage—is the smooth, pinkish bole of a large angophora (a species of native tree closely related to the eucalyptus). Beyond are banks of azaleas and cotoneasters, flourishing alongside the dramatic shapes of canna lilies and red-hot pokers. The geometrically shaped beds are filled with whatever flowers are in season—zinnias, dahlias, asters, Iceland poppies. Most important are the copious varieties of rose, classical favourites that have taken well to the soil of Sydney—although they can become overblown in the steamy summer heat.

An English acquaintance of mine visiting Sydney complained of the lack of restraint reflected in what he described as the enamelled garishness of Sydney gardens; but I take unashamed pleasure in looking out on a backyard that includes both jacaranda and honeysuckle, prickly pear and wisteria; and where, for that matter, Indian mynah birds and English sparrows (both species originally imported in the 1860s to keep down the caterpillar population) compete with indigenous magpies, kookaburras and crow-like currawongs.

Because the private gardens are so ubiquitous, Sydney has less need than most European cities for spacious municipal parks. Even so, downtown Sydney is provided with two green areas incorporating the Botanic Gardens, the Domain and Hyde Park (adjoining each other), and Moore and Centennial parks two miles further to the south-east. There are also scattered areas of land around the entrance to Sydney Harbour that are reserved as bushland and provide walks for the few Sydneysiders who realize that such treasures are there. On the north shore, for example, on the Woolwich Peninsula at the mouth of the Lane Cove River, there are eight acres of wild, waterfront property known as Kelly's Bush. Further east, more bushland adjoins the Taronga ("beautiful view") Park Zoo— aptly named, since the zoo occupies a spectacular site sloping down towards the harbour; from one of the wharfs on Circular Quay you can buy a combined ferry-zoo ticket for an excursion across the water to visit it.

Most important of all, Sydney is flanked by several enormous national parks. Within a 60-mile radius of Sydney, about 20 per cent of the land is preserved. On the city's Pacific seaboard, 15 miles south of Circular Quay, lies the Royal National Park, nearly 37,000 acres of forest. Almost as large is Ku-ring-gai Chase National Park to the north. Established towards the

In the Ku-ring-gai Chase National Park, 57 square miles of bushland on Sydney's northern perimeter, just 10 miles from the city centre, an exposed slab of sandstone bears Aboriginal engravings of unknown date. The images depict a hunter (background) and his quarry of large and small fishes; the outline enclosing the small fish may represent a human form. More than 600 groups of rock-cut figures, believed by their makers to bring success in hunting, have been found in the region of Sydney.

Members of one of Sydney's many keen bushwalking clubs on a day's hike through the Royal National Park stop to make a hot drink by boiling their billycans over a wood-fire in time-honoured style (left), before pushing on through a spring shower (right). Camp-fires are not forbidden except in the summer period of exceptionally high temperatures when the risk of bush-fires is extreme.

end of the 19th Century, these two parks were originally regarded as "useless" land, being then some distance from the city outskirts and not suited to agriculture because of the thin, poor soil. Today they serve a purpose unforeseen by their founders: they act as barriers to urban sprawl. Without the parks, Sydney's suburbs might by now have joined those of the industrial cities of Newcastle to the north and Wollongong to the south, to create a megalopolis. Brisbane Water Park (encompassing nearly 20,000 acres across Broken Bay from Ku-ring-gai Chase) and Dharug National Park, a 35,000-acre virgin wilderness that is renowned for its Aboriginal symbols engraved on the rocks, are also to the north, some 30 miles away from the city centre.

"Bushwalking"—hiking for pleasure through Sydney's bush country—has a long history; it has been popular since the 1890s. The city has numerous enthusiastic bushwalking clubs, whose activities take place in one or another of the national parks, or along the meandering reaches of the Hawkesbury and McDonald rivers to the north, or further west along the Nepean River or among the Blue Mountains, of which an area of some 500,000 acres is also classified as a national park.

My own experience of the Sydney bush is mostly of the Sunday-afternoon-at-Ku-ring-gai-Chase variety. The first sight of the car parks at the most popular recreation areas can be daunting, since they betray the presence of hundreds of similarly minded escapees. At West Head, at Cottage Point and at Bobbin Head—the three most remote locations at Ku-ring-gai Chase that are accessible by car—many of the less intrepid spirits are not energetic enough to stray very far from their vehicles; but others take the winding trails into the bush. You do not have to walk for long to gain the illusion that you are nowhere near a great city: the bush

has a way of covering up the presence of humans, and even succeeds in concealing modern tin cans and packaging detritus, as though it were shyly obeying the rules of ecology and tidiness. In these primeval spaces, it almost seems as if every foreign object is biodegradable.

Sydney's national parks are being saved from the worst ravages of picnickers and barbecue-fanciers by the careful planning of campsites, so as to keep them from spreading unnecessarily or occupying prominent positions. The parks' permanent residents—the thousands of native species of fauna and flora—are protected by law. Wallabies may sometimes be seen scampering into the bush before you as you walk, and among the more conspicuous animals are goannas—large but harmless lizards of frighteningly prehistoric appearance, whose popular Australian name is a corruption of "iguana"—and possums. These latter thick-furred tree-dwellers with their long prehensile tails are familiar, too, in those outlying areas of Sydney that are near bush country; they are good scavengers that come out in the evening and can be seen strolling around in suburban gardens. Sometimes they even wander into houses. If surprised indoors, they are less welcome, since they panic when approached and react by biting and scratching.

Snakes, fortunately, are not very common sights in the national parks, for they harbour quite as much fear of man as man does of them and slither rapidly away. Nor are koalas at all frequently found, except in the special sanctuaries maintained for them. Koalas are placid animals, very sensitive to changes in the environment, and are particularly wary of cars. They are finicky about food too; they eat only a select variety of eucalyptus leaves. The park visitor may spot a koala aloft in a gum tree, picturesquely munching its staple diet. Eucalyptus leaves are popularly but wrongly thought to contain a sedative ingredient, to account for the koala's permanent appearance of mild stupor; in fact the animal looks bleary by day because it is a mainly nocturnal creature.

Some of the most enjoyable sights of the parks are small and secretive. Where there is flowing water, there is life. The narrow creeks that drain the bush may occur as frequently as every hundred yards. Along their banks the subdued stars of wild flowers colour the heat of the day. Lizards bake on boulders no more than an inch or two above the trickling water. The watercourses themselves are sometimes so slow that they seem merely to be linked ponds; at other times they race over smooth, shallow beds. From the cave-pitted banks of the darker river valleys emerge bats, to flap blindly around your head.

You need be no ornithologist to enjoy the flamboyant plumage sported by Australia's birds—the scarlets, sulphurs and indigos mixed together by nature, which need not be inhibited by the dictates of either fashion or sobriety. The native birds—the rosellas, honey-eaters, whip-birds (long-tailed, with a loud whip-crack call) and many others—can be seen at their

Many of the Australian continent's unique animals and birds are protected in the national parks within easy motoring distance of Sydney. Shown here are a kookaburra (left), a koala (right) and a pair of great grey kangaroos (below).

best in the bush; but you must be quick, as they dart through the light-leaved trees or keep low in the ferny scrub at your feet.

As to insect and spider life, it is prodigious and even somewhat alarming. Spiders often spin their webs across the space between shrubs on either side of a bush path, and so you find yourself confronting webs face-first a dozen times in the course of an afternoon's walk. The webs are sometimes so thick that you cannot pass until you have dislodged them with the aid of a strong stick.

One of the most comforting sounds known to me is a peculiarity of the bush, the gentle and continuous noise of water in descent through the hot extent of the scrubland. Stop still for a moment and you can tune into a miasma of sound that is incessant, an assertion that nature will not be disturbed by the presence of man.

The bush, rather reassuringly, is never silent. Even in Sydney itself, insects insist on adding to the universal cacophony. On the harbour the cicadas are as well drilled as an army of cheer-leaders. As if at a signal, thousands of them will begin shrilling, and will maintain their wall of ringing sound for hours on end; then, just as suddenly, they will all stop at once, as if a switch had been thrown.

The beauty of the Australian bush, as one Sydney bushwalking addict explained it to me, is its timelessness—a landscape, uniquely close to a major metropolis, that has remained unchanged for thousands of years. Nor, for that matter, does the average bushwalker have any desire to change it; at heart he is almost certainly a conservationist. It is understandable that men and women who have felt the hostility of their surroundings should retain mixed feelings about the bush, and that to them the conservationists' love-hymns may not sound altogether sweet. But the ecology lobby in Australia is strong, although monitored and kept practical by inborn Australian scepticism.

The start of one of the most remarkable conservation movements anywhere was the rescue of Kelly's Bush from "development" in June 1971. It was a battle that made Australian history. When it was discovered that 25 luxury homes were planned for the area, a pressure group of 13 local housewives in the affluent suburb of Hunter's Hill—they called themselves the "Battlers for Kelly's Bush"—fought vigorously against the re-zoning of the land as a residential district. Leading officials of the New South Wales Builders' Labourers Federation (the B.L.F.) were soon giving their support and promised that their members would refuse to contribute their labour to any building project on Kelly's Bush. The alliance between the upper-middle-class matrons and the left-wing union bosses may have been incongruous but it was effective.

In subsequent confrontations the ecology movement's muscle came largely from the B.L.F. working in conjunction with various other local con-

Dating from the 19th Century, Waverley cemetery occupies a rugged cliffside once considered worthless land, but now engulfed by a tide of suburban homes.

servation groups; the labour union effected so-called "green bans" on more than 40 sites where new—and in the conservationists' view—unwarranted construction had been proposed. The term "green ban" was the brainchild of Jack Mundey, the Secretary of the B.L.F. in 1971. "There's building that needs to be done, but a lot that doesn't," he said at the time. "I don't want my son to accuse me of helping to destroy Sydney. Our generation has options—and his should, too." It was a bolder stance than many Australians might then have been prepared to take up.

In the early days of the green bans, there were some unexpected detractors. The *Sydney Morning Herald* commented ungenerously in an editorial: "There is something highly comical in the spectacle of builders' labourers, whose ideas on industrial relations do not rise above strikes, violence, intimidation and the destruction of property, setting themselves up as arbiters of taste and protectors of our national heritage." It was predicted that pro-conservation bans imposed by unions could not survive periods of economic difficulty and high unemployment. In fact, the ecology lobby gathered momentum throughout the 1970s, and the Sydney authorities themselves steadily became much more sympathetic towards appeals against unaesthetic urban development.

Not all the conservationists' energies have been directed towards the preservation of Sydney's open spaces and its historic buildings. The city has been the scene of marches on such national issues as the mining of rutile (the ore from which titanium—a metal used in the aerospace industry—is extracted), which was defacing the beautiful beaches of Fraser Island, 150 miles north of Brisbane; Aboriginal land rights; and the chopping-down of virgin forests to feed the Japanese hi-fi industry's insatiable appetite for chipboard facias. Ecology has become a national movement and many of its leading Sydney supporters are highly vocal. Espousers have ranged from trade-union leaders to university professors of botany and biology, and leading literary figures such as poet Judith Wright and novelist Patrick White.

Centennial Park, the city's largest, was protected by a green ban in 1972, after plans had been mooted for a huge Olympic-size sports ground to be built on part of it, and on the neighbouring Moore Park. Public protest led to an official inquiry that recommended against the use of the park for the complex. Subsequently, less was heard of the New South Wales government's scheme to attract the 1988 Olympic Games to Sydney.

Perhaps, after all, public care for the welfare of the natural world is not so strange in a country where literature and art are preoccupied with nature and its opposition to man to a degree hardly paralleled in any other country. Nature is the Great Australian Muse.

From the beginning, incipient Australian poets and novelists had to find ways of acclimatizing themselves to the isolation and provincialism of colonial life. They had much to learn. As late as the 1920s one Sydney poet, Hugh McCrae, became known for his poems devoted to peopling the bush around Sydney with dryads, nymphs and centaurs. But though his verses enjoyed a temporary popularity, the incongruity of European spirits cavorting in the unfamiliar Australian undergrowth eventually dissipated their mythic force. Nature—real Australian nature—quickly became, and still remains, the main protagonist of Australian literature. Fundamental to it is a prevailing sense of a force that is larger than human will, and indifferent to morality and petition. Even Patrick White, Australia's most distinguished writer, was only awarded the accolade of his country-men's special admiration after he had produced a nature saga. To have written *The Tree of Man* (a tale of soul-crinkling deprivation on a small farm between the two world wars) and *Voss* (an allegory of the inner Australian emptiness) gave White a standing that the Nobel Prize for Literature could not have conferred alone.

For Australia's artists, confronted with a multitude of unknown forms, it was necessary in the early days to discover how to draw and paint afresh: gum trees and the unfamiliar hues of the bush were hard to render if your ideal of nature was the comfortable English oaks painted by John Constable, or the brooding Germanic forests of Caspar David Friedrich. In the 19th Century, artists often strove to fit the harsh and daunting reality of Australia into the mould of traditional European beauty and conventional theories of the picturesque; but around the turn of the century, Australia's great recorders of the natural scene, Arthur Streeton and Tom Roberts, revolutionized Australian painting with their impressionistic renderings of the country's brightly sunlit landscape. Their attempts to capture on canvas the unusual tones and colours of their land owed as much to their love of Australian nature as it did to their desire to create a truly distinctive—and national—school of art.

Among the most successful of all representations of the unique qualities of the Australian countryside are the landscapes of Arthur Boyd. A member of a prominent Australian artistic family, Boyd became one of the country's most distinguished painters during the 1950s. His versions of the countryside near Melbourne and the River Wimmera tellingly impart the light, dry and golden tone of the bush; but his later works—painted since he settled in 1975 on the Shoalhaven River about a hundred miles south of Sydney—are something more: he has found a technical vocabulary and a range of colour tones that perfectly represent the hard, high light and the straw-coloured grasses, the laminated blue-brown of the river, and above all the deep recesses of the pencil-slim eucalypts rising in a thousand spoke-like lines upon the wooded hills.

Boyd's work is in great demand among collectors, in Sydney and else-where, and, inevitably, his paintings are bought by the rich as investments and tax hedges—though I am sure that such buyers also genuinely love

November clouds glow over the Sydney skyline at sunset. Though summer rainstorms can be torrential, the land is soon parched again by the scorching sun.

the reflections of their country that they find in Boyd's art. He has built for himself a beautiful house on the banks of the Shoalhaven, where I once went with my children to spend a weekend with him. He met us at the station at Nowra—the nearest railhead to his house—and drove us in a Land-Rover along an almost impassable track torn out of the bush by bull-dozers. The house, situated on a sweeping bend of the wide river, was designed by a Chinese architect from Canberra, and reproduces the wide verandas and galvanized roof of the old settlers' homes. It is quite isolated —an "electrified redoubt" with every sophisticated comfort, but out of sight of all other human habitation—and, as I stood, glass in hand, on the broad front veranda looking downriver towards the sea, I was startled by the sudden appearance of water-skiers, as if from the middle of nowhere, creaming up the broad expanse of water. But once they had passed, we were left again with the quiet pastoral view: the broad and sand-banked curves of the superb river, the soaring gulls, and the crop-filled pelicans.

Boyd has painted many versions of the surrounding countryside and of the forested hills sloping down to the wide stretches of water. He is equally happy rowing across the river to paint with dervish obsession the vista of his house beneath its protective wooded hill, or tramping through the nearby forest to point out a rare orchid, or exploring the small creeks that trickle down the wild hillsides.

He observed to me that the indifference and emptiness of Australia bring out in its inhabitants a sense of the imprisonment and violence of their own natures. And I realized, then, that of all the population, it is Australia's painters who are most at home in, and with, the wilderness; they do not set themselves against it, nor do they wring from it anything other than understanding.

Even if they cannot match Boyd's marvellous union of wildness and modernity, many people choose to live—as it were—both *in* and *out* of Sydney; to enjoy the advantages of metropolitan services and yet spend more of their time closer to nature than most townspeople can. In Sydney, you can live in a beach-house near the sea and yet still be within an hour's commuting distance of Circular Quay, or you can buy (or build) a retreat in Sydney's "hill stations" in the Blue Mountains, and travel to it by railway or automobile—or even commute daily to and from work in Sydney. You can find a small farm or establish a craft shop; cottage industries are returning to Sydney's outermost areas, as potters, artists and others seek-ing to escape from urban life move out of the city, hoping to make a living from the ecology boom and the revulsion from mass-produced goods. Sydney people like not only to look at nature but to photograph it, paint it, classify it: the Blue Mountains teem with artists and every sizeable township there boasts several galleries where local inhabitants display their creative efforts. Many refugees from commercialism have made their homes in beautiful old settlements such as Mittagong and Berrima, 70 or 80 miles from Sydney. The first of these has a biennial music festival, during which it is a special delight to hear the sound of a string quartet or some snatch of polyphony wafting through the upland wattles.

Beethoven headed the first movement of his Pastoral Symphony "Awakening of pleasant feelings upon arriving in the country". Most Sydney-dwellers would share that sensation; like Beethoven, they are indubitably townspeople, but it is with an anticipatory quickening of the spirit that the Sydneysider packs his car on a Friday afternoon to set out westwards to his retreat—his Blue Mountain cottage in Katoomba (largest of the mountain townships) or Leura or Blackheath. Once there, he checks to see if the possums have caused any damage to his roof or veranda, and hopes against hope that the smoke from bush-fires he sees against the fast-fading light, and rolling up the valley, is travelling in the opposite direction.

If he has made good time on the journey—and if he's feeling too tired to use the ultra-modern oven in his expensive kitchen—he may decide to take his wife out to dinner. After a telephone call to reserve a table at one of the many restaurants specializing in *haute cuisine*, they will set off again in the car for a journey of 10 miles or more, to dine expensively on trout from the local streams, garlic bread and *coq au vin*, accompanied by the best New South Wales wines from the Hunter Valley.

Next morning, he will probably wake to the shrill, laughing cry of a kookaburra in the trees by his bedroom and make an inspection of his modest estate. At around 3,000 feet, the Blue Mountains are just high enough to encourage imported trees and shrubs of the temperate sort. He will check the progress of his rhododendrons and oak tree saplings. He will be even more concerned for the rare native plants that he may be coaxing through the trauma of transplantation. At breakfast, the radio tells him of local bush-fire movements and the likely maximum temperature of the day ahead. Perhaps the family will decide to pack a lunch for a picnic in one of the hundreds of small creek valleys that radiate from the mountain spur, or to set out on a longer and more difficult walk along trails that no car can follow.

Once they plunge down into the Blue Mountains' rain-forest they are back in the Carboniferous and Triassic ages of some 150 million years ago. This is a vegetable kingdom—a world ruled by plants, with their own tricks for survival. The mountains trap the rainfall and send the overflow down into the valleys through thousands of runnels and channels. As it cascades and reticulates, it topples hundreds of feet over dark-green escarpments; it gushes through rock pipeways as cunningly contrived by nature as the conduits of a Renaissance pleasure-garden; it lies reflectively in sunlit shallows on which leaves float in miniature regattas.

The sense of being back in an older world is enhanced by the predominance of ferns among the plants of the mountainside. Ferns were kings before the dinosaurs and they still dominate the darker, wetter parts of the bush. Sometimes one happens on an exotic orchid battening on a rock face, or gripping the slimy walls of one of the many small waterfalls that abound in the mountains.

By way of contrast, the Blue Mountains also foster a small tourist industry of visitors from the rest of Australia. They take the precipitous funicular railway down the gorge beside the Three Sisters rock formation, drag their children away from the railings above the blue-rinsed depths of the ravine at Govett's Leap, and set out by the busload to inspect the stalactites, stalagmites and other artificially illuminated subterranean wonders of the Jenolan Caves, a sandstone formation 110 miles west of Sydney in the Blue Mountains National Park.

The Blue Mountains are beautiful but, to my mind, they are more picturesque than awe-inspiring, as low key as the air-cooled silver trains that wind their dignified way up into the mountain resorts, bringing some thousands of visitors a year, especially in the summer holiday season. Little in this area is spectacular; yet, although nature manages to keep herself in restraint, every inch of this land belongs, undoubtedly, to her.

Even in these regions, apparently so unthreatening, when all gold drains from the landscape at the end of the afternoon, a more sinister green sets in, and the Sydneysider's thoughts begin to turn citywards again. Driving back to Sydney after the weekend, he welcomes the re-assurance he finds in the company of his fellows. He has enjoyed his excursion into nature, but he is still glad to turn his face again towards the great man-made city, and to rejoin the urban majority.

6

A Hearty Taste for the Good Life

On any day in the Australian summer—that is from late October to early April—an aerial view of Sydney presents a panorama of one of the biggest and busiest playgrounds on earth. Below, on the 36 ocean beaches that lie within the city limits, ant-like hordes of people are gathered to sunbathe, swim and ride the boiling surf. The sails of countless pleasure boats, large and small, criss-cross the waters of Sydney Harbour in bewildering array. Then, turning inshore, the eye discerns an infinite number of green or brown ovals, squares and rectangles, each indicating some area where Sydneysiders—cricket lovers, racegoers, tennis players, golfers, lawn bowlers, picnickers—are busily sharing their notion of "the good life".

Most great cities of the world undergo a fairly dramatic change in lifestyle as their inhabitants end the working week and turn to leisure pursuits. In Sydney, however, every day in summer has something of a weekend quality —for two reasons. Firstly, the city offers an impressive wealth and range of outdoor recreational amenities within its metropolitan area. Secondly, Sydneysiders are unmatched in their relentless determination to extract maximum pleasure from their free time. Not without some reason has it been said that the average working man in Sydney considers his employment to be an irritating interruption of his leisure.

To a degree, this determination to take their ease characterizes Australians in general. As an Australian writer, Craig McGregor, has expressed it: "In the end Australians prefer having a good time to anything else. It's the pleasures of life—sunshine, beer and sex—which count, not the responsibilities. Existence is not for achieving something but simply for enjoying." This preference manifests itself in Sydney, above all Australian cities. Here, the passion for leisure pursuits can, very logically, be attributed to Sydney's magnificent climate and geographical position. When a place is endowed with so many basic elements for pleasurable outdoor recreation, it is perfectly natural that its people should value—and indeed expect— time to enjoy these gifts.

For most Sydneysiders, the focus of the good life is, inevitably, the shore. All the way from Botany Bay up to Barranjoey Head, 36 miles north, lie the beaches that have made swimming and surfing the obsession of the masses. Their names are part of Sydney mythology: Cronulla, Maroubra, Coogee, Clovelly, Bondi, Curl Curl and Dee Why, Collaroy, Narrabeen, Mona Vale, Avalon, Whale Beach.

It is true that there are some 90 species of shark in Australian waters; and sensationalists spin yarns about encounters with 750-pound specimens.

Two players collide in a first-division Rugby League match between teams representing the suburbs of Cronulla and Manly. The professional League draws larger Sydney crowds than any other winter sport. Local supporters of each club belong to large-scale organizations whose luxurious premises provide wide-ranging recreational facilities for their members.

But the danger—except in shark-infested Sydney Harbour—is minimal. Only a handful are of the man-eating variety and rarely will any venture close to shore. In fact, the overwhelming majority of swimmers in Sydney have never seen a shark except in the Aquarium at Manly, and some of those who claim to have seen a "real killer" will actually have encountered nothing more than a dolphin's fin. Though rare, dolphins are still a much more familiar sight than sharks; they are so playful that they sometimes bob up alongside a surfer to join him in catching a wave.

Over the years, of course, Sydney has occasionally known some horrifying shark attacks—enough to prompt the authorities to institute routine air-and-sea patrols (either bells or sirens sound a warning on beaches as soon as sharks are spotted), and to have net barriers laid down to protect many of the beaches. Personally, I would rate my chances of being attacked by a shark off a Sydney beach as no higher than my chances of winning one of the state lotteries. A far greater nuisance to swimmers, I would say, are the Portuguese men-of-war—a kind of jellyfish that can be a plague upon the city's coastline. Their poisonous sting, though easily counteracted, is extremely uncomfortable.

Bondi, which alone lures almost three million people every summer, is commercialized as well as crowded. However, it is the city's most accessible surf beach, a mere 15-minute drive from the city centre and, therefore, from Sydney's earliest days, it has been Australia's most renowned and popular seaside playground (probably only Hawaii's Waikiki is equally familiar worldwide as a beach name). Still, especially at weekends, some Sydney families prefer to drive out further to quieter and less frequented beaches.

During the summer months the Bondi day begins around 6 a.m. when the official beach inspector arrives to make his expert assessment of the prevailing tides and currents. Soon afterwards, the early morning ocean addicts and joggers begin to arrive, to enjoy themselves exercising for an hour or so before going home for breakfast and the start of the working day. During the week, the mothers with young families begin to come on the scene after breakfast. Within a few hours the thousand-yard-long beach is predominantly occupied by bikini-clad mums reading paperbacks, and their small children, who splash in the shallows or sit about building sand-castles. Inevitably, during the school summer holidays, the beach is far more noisy and crowded. And at weekends and on public holidays, the scene is positively chaotic. It can seem as though all of Sydney has congregated on Bondi's 75,000 square yards of fine-grained white sand.

The weekend crowds are divided by the aquatic conditions into three separate groups, according to whether the roughest waves are coming in at the north or south end of the bay. The middle of the beach, where the waters are usually most tranquil, is mainly occupied by swimmers of moderate ability and by would-be body-surfers seeking to catch a mild wave. The calmer end is favoured by children big enough to use a surfoplane (an

Team members from one of Sydney's many volunteer life-saving clubs fasten their surf-caps before carrying out a simulated rescue operation on Bondi Beach.

Aspiring young life-savers take instruction in the prescribed drill for falling into line. At 13, they will be eligible to join a club for advanced training.

inflatable rubber float) but too small and inexperienced to use a proper surf-board. The end where the waves are biggest is the preserve of experienced surf-board riders, many of them teenagers who, with their deeply bronzed skin and salt-bleached hair, look as though they have spent their entire youth in the sea and sun.

On almost any summer's day at Bondi, you are likely to see beach guards make a dramatic dash to save someone who has been toppled from a surf-oplane after venturing too far out to sea. It was on this beach that Australia's great life-saving movement was born in 1906. A group of Sydney citizens formed the Bondi Surf Bathers' Life Saving Club, with a view to reducing the high incidence of drownings that occurred largely as a result of swimmers failing to recognize the danger from tremendously powerful rip-tides. Similar clubs were formed subsequently on other beaches and soon they were all united under a central controlling body, the Surf Life Saving Association of Australia.

The Association today has about 120 clubs in New South Wales, and in Sydney itself there are more than 3,500 active members—as well as another 2,000 who can be called out in emergencies. It is an entirely voluntary organization that receives some financial support from the government. The Association's National Council co-ordinates fund-raising programmes and the development of new life-saving techniques and equipment. Membership, on payment of a minimal annual subscription, is open to young people over 13 years of age, who, after an extensive training curriculum that includes development of surfing, rowing, rescue and resuscitation skills, must pass an examination in order to qualify for taking part in life-saving beach patrols. Successful completion of the training course is marked by the award of a bronze medal.

At the times when the shores are most crowded—such as summer evenings, weekends and school holidays—life-savers in teams of about eight patrol the beaches. At these times red-and-yellow flags are flown to indicate the areas being patrolled, which are therefore safe for bathing.

There are no financial rewards for the dedicated life-savers who watch Sydney's beaches. They are compensated instead by the prestige of their role, by comradeship and pride of achievement (they can compete with other life-savers for silver and gold medals in inter-club contests), and by the advantages of having access to beachside clubhouses with facilities for changing and storage space for their surf-boards and equipment. There is no upper age limit to membership of the clubs, but beyond the age of 36 life-savers are required to pass an annual fitness test.

Today, on all of Sydney's surfing beaches, the surf life-saving movement is still prominently in evidence. The bronzed praetorian life-guards stand ready in their red-and-yellow skull-caps, designed to make them easily identifiable to the public, and conspicuous when only their heads bob above the waves. The traditional bathing-suits, with club insignia, that they

At a suburban tennis club, where Saturday morning coaching sessions are regularly attended by more than 60 schoolchildren, a professional takes a young novice by stages through the correct body co-ordination for serving. Sydney's well-organized coaching programmes, plus its wealth of public and private courts, have contributed greatly to Australia's world prominence in tennis.

wear when competing or giving life-saving demonstrations, have—to the foreign eye—a prudish, old-fashioned look, but the shoulder straps were designed to hold a suit on even in the roughest waves. There are the steel towers from which the patrols maintain a constant vigil for sharks; there are the reels of strong line that can be attached to a life-guard's harness; there are the varnished and polished club surf-boats, half-way between ship's cutters and Viking long ships, drawn up on the sand or nosing out from the boat-house. And throughout the day, by means of loudspeakers, the life-savers' clubhouse broadcasts announcements and beach safety warnings.

Almost every weekend, from December to March, clubs from the different beaches stage surf carnivals. These occasions begin with the traditional opening parade: lines of barrel-chested life-guards, dressed in their full swimming regalia, resplendent in colours and badges, marching behind their respective club banners with the curious high-stepping style designed to keep step on soft sand. Then the clubs compete in a variety of swimming and boat races. Six-man belt-and-reel squads are judged on their speed and precision in spilling a lifeline, securing it to a club member in the role of swimmer in distress, hauling him back to safety, then carrying out artificial respiration. And invariably the most exciting event of the carnival is a race among five-man boat teams: four oarsmen and a helmsman. At the firing of a starting pistol the crews drag out their wooden lifeboats and then struggle to manoeuvre them through gigantic breakers to distant marker-buoys and back to the beach again.

Yet, in spite of their vigorous presence, Sydney's life-savers no longer enjoy the great glamour and prestige they once commanded. All through the 1930s and 1940s, competition to join the life-saving clubs was intense; membership meant that you belonged to a hard-working and hard-drinking élite, and when you were out on patrol you were automatically one of the kings of the beach. Not so today. Indeed, some life-saving clubs now go through periods of being under strength—a circumstance that would have been unthinkable a few decades ago.

The decline dates from the 1950s when the so-called "surfie" culture—originating in the United States—found a natural new home in Sydney. At first, the "surfie" was defined as a kind of beach beatnik. Subsequently, however, the cult acquired a degree of respectability; in 1964 Midget Farrelly, a skinny 23-year-old from New South Wales, became Australia's first world champion surfer and an idol of his generation. Since then, the sport has boomed so greatly that Sydney alone is estimated to have more than 250,000 enthusiasts. As a result, its superstars now enjoy the kind of admiration and respect that was once the monopoly of the life-guards.

Nowadays, when so many old traditions and values are being challenged, there is a growing tendency among young Australians to see the skull-capped, high-stepping life-guards as overgrown boy scouts obsessed with performing good deeds, winning badges of merit and preserving old rituals. Yet the importance of Sydney's life-savers has never been greater, since more people than ever before are sporting off the city's beaches.

Perhaps none of the "surfies" is old enough to have first-hand memories of "Black Sunday", February 6, 1938, the day when Bondi's beach patrollers most nobly lived up to their motto "Vigilance and Service". On that sunny afternoon, when the beach was especially crowded, there suddenly crashed without warning four huge freak waves—up to 25 feet high—followed by such a powerful undertow that people were bathing from a sandbank near the beach one moment and the next floundering in the deep out of reach of the shore. Altogether, some 200 people were swept out to sea. But no fewer than 50 life-guards were at hand, and they acted so swiftly and heroically that only four bathers drowned and two were missing.

Today, no less, Sydney's life-saving clubs are well equipped to tackle major emergencies. They may preserve old-fashioned gear for the sake of tradition, but they also possess highly efficient new equipment that was unavailable on that horrifying "Black Sunday"—motor-powered rescue boats of sophisticated design, plus (since 1973) a Helicopter Rescue Service, sponsored by the Bank of New South Wales and manned by a 40-strong team of doctors, scuba divers, and first-aid and resuscitation officers.

There are only five months in the year, May to September, when Sydney's life-saving volunteers can relax their vigilance. Then, as the average air temperature falls to 57°F, the beaches are relatively deserted. Keep-fit enthusiasts still appear every morning to go jogging, or to work out in the gymnasium of a beachside life-saving club. But only a limited number of Spartans—like the members of the Bondi Icebergs Club, a winter swimming association formed in 1929—continue to take their regular dip in the somewhat chilly waters.

However, even in winter, the sea remains one of Sydney's foremost attractions, for this is a city with more than 50,000 pleasure craft, and Sydneysiders are never more themselves than when they are "messing about in boats". All year round Sydney Harbour is crowded with vessels of every conceivable shape and size, from tiny dinghies manned by 11-year-olds to streamlined powerboats and great ocean-racing yachts. The demand for moorings in the harbour is so excessive that a registration system is strictly enforced to prevent hopeless congestion.

The most famous event in Sydney's crowded yachting calendar is the 630-mile race from the harbour to Hobart in Tasmania. First instituted in 1945, the contest always starts on the morning of December 26, and can continue, depending on weather conditions, into the first week of January. It is not the longest of great ocean races, but it is certainly one of the most spectacular, since it is not unusual for the yachts to encounter gale-force winds, strong cross-currents, and even schools of whales.

Yacht racing in Sydney Harbour is highly organized and classified, ranging from events for dinghies (between 12 and 18 feet) to ocean-going craft (more than 30 feet). The most beautiful class, to my mind—and also the most popular—are the 18-foot skiffs. These sailing boats are undecked, can take a crew of up to a dozen, and carry a mainsail, one or more jibs and an enormous spinnaker for running before the wind. Their deep centreboard makes them so manoeuvrable that, as they tack, they can lean in the wind until the mast almost touches the surface of the water.

On a clear summer's afternoon, the sight of competing 18-footers offers a brilliant enticement to the eye as they skim over the blue water, their bright-coloured spinnakers bellying and the crew members, only their toes touching the gunwale, leaning out on trapezes to balance them. Whenever they are racing, thousands of spectators follow behind in special ferry boats, where betting on the outcome of the race, although illegal, is carried on with feverish intensity.

In theory, anyone with a boat can relax by sailing in the harbour; on most summer days the waters are relatively calm, and the courses being used by the racing yachtsmen are clearly marked by buoys. In practice, however, I have sometimes found sailing in the harbour to be positively unnerving, and about as enjoyable as crossing Pitt Street, perhaps Sydney's busiest road, against the rush-hour traffic.

I remember especially making a cautious trip out of the Rose Bay marina in a small sailing craft skippered by a doctor friend of mine. Almost

Cricket enthusiasts—lightly dressed for comfort in the blazing sun, many with their portable ice-boxes beside them—sit jammed together on "the Hill", a grassy bank in the 65,000-capacity Sydney Cricket Ground. Many of Australia's international Test matches are played there against such opponents as England, the West Indies, India or Pakistan. Local fans become especially vociferous when Australia faces her traditional cricket rival, England (bowler, above).

immediately after leaving our mooring we found ourselves in the path of a phalanx of racing yachts. By dint of frantic manoeuvring, we avoided them and headed for mid-harbour. We hoped to sail two and a half miles west towards Fort Denison and then head under the Sydney Harbour Bridge towards the halcyon waters of Balmain and the entrance to the Parramatta River. But in mid-channel we encountered another dashing cavalcade of large yachts, voluptuous spinnakers billowing before them, bearing down directly upon us. We tacked, we jibbed; but wherever we went, the great vessels cut across and behind us like torpedoes and as though deliberately aimed to miss us by only a fraction. Finally we abandoned all hope of passing under the bridge. Instead, we fled south to the safe waters of Rushcutters Bay, and there, mooring some hundred yards from shore, gradually regained our composure as we picnicked on Greek olives, pepperoni salami and French bread, washed down with plenty of Hunter Valley Riesling. Sailing in Sydney Harbour, I have since concluded, is best enjoyed as a spectator.

I have already alluded to the relentless determination that Sydneysiders bring to their pursuit of pleasure. And the objective word is "pursuit"; there is a sense of urgency and purpose about this chase which, as I see it, tends to vitiate true, spontaneous joyfulness.

The poet Les Murray—perhaps the most persuasive of the nationalist school of writers who, in the 1960s, devoted themselves to establishing an identifiably Australian literature—has described his countrymen's pursuit of happiness in terms of a tribal and ritual activity. And certainly this aspect of Australian-style hedonism is strongly in evidence during Sydney's summer weekends. Mother packs the "Esky" (a large portable ice-box, named after the trademark of the original Eskimo brand) with steaks and sausages, coleslaw and drinks; father prepares the barbecue equipment; and the kids assemble their various bats and balls. Then they all pile into the family station wagon and head out to one of the many barbecue sites around the city centre, where they light a fire, grill their steaks, and picnic and play for hours in the sun.

It is a pleasant enough family scene, a style of organized outing that citizens living in less equable climes might very well envy. Nevertheless, I still gain the impression that this kind of leisure activity often involves a disciplined purposefulness that exacts its own price, as though the pursuit of happiness were not merely an inalienable right, but almost an obligatory duty—the business of "having a good time" not permitting abstention.

I know of no other city where there is so much organization of fun—on the family level or by way of Sydney's many thousands of sports or social clubs. Inside each Sydneysider there seems to be a "Chairman of the Activities Committee" who feels it is his duty to conscript everyone around him into playing some part in the great game of finding pleasure. This is not to suggest that Sydney is predominantly populated by sports-playing, keep-fit fanatics. It has more than its fair share of sporting duffers and there are still quite a few pot-bellied ockers who will tackle nothing more strenuous than lifting a schooner of ale. But neither sporting ineptitude nor physical deficiency excuses a Sydneysider from devotion to some casual activity or other—whether it be supporting a cricket or Rugby football team, going with friends to the race-track, planning barbecue outings, or simply organizing poker games. He need not be an active sportsman, but he should never, ever, be a "spoil-sport".

Sydney, of course, is renowned throughout the world as a great centre of sport, and its range of sporting facilities is outstanding. At the same time, it is to be noted that the watching of sport, rather than the playing of it, is the dominant activity for the vast majority of Sydneysiders. It is time to bury the great myth that the ambition of every true Australian is to become an international sports star; that every one of its major cities teems with competitive youngsters who, urged on by equally competitive parents or Svengali-like coaches, and in the cherished hope of becoming a champion, are swimming, or running and jumping, or kicking and bowling balls, or swinging rackets, bats and clubs.

The origin of the myth is easily identified. It was born in the late 1950s during the course of a decade in which Australia, in spite of its relatively small population, suddenly and miraculously began to spawn champions, both male and female. Rarely in the history of sport has there been such a spectacularly quick advance by one nation on so many different sporting fronts, especially tennis, track and field events and, above all, swimming.

Why did Australia's sporting boom occur when it did? It was the result of a number of favourable circumstances coinciding. Most importantly, the post-Second World War economic growth enabled cities to begin providing a wealth of facilities: new running tracks, public tennis courts and swimming pools, more golf courses, cricket and Rugby grounds. The Olympic Games were held in Melbourne in 1956, and Australia was especially fortunate in the 1950s in having enlightened sports administrators and an exceptional number of outstanding coaches. As a result, the best possible use was made of the country's young sporting talent, and Australians warmly welcomed their success as a way of asserting their youthful country's importance before the world at large.

In the 1960s Australians continued to figure prominently in world sport—most especially in lawn tennis. But the country's swimmers and athletes were not quite so dominant, and in the 1970s Australia's command even of world tennis began to evaporate. What caused the decline? I believe one need not look beyond Sydney's affluent and plentiful present-day leisure scene to perceive a major part of the explanation. At weekends in summer, the heavy traffic on the beach roads includes carloads of young swimmers who, with surf-boards stacked high on the roof of their Holden, are cruising

A Rugby supporter's crocheted hat, adorned with plastic-covered beer labels, proclaims his taste for ale.

The Art of Beer-Drinking

It has been said that beer is a religion in Australia. And research confirms that the dedication of Australians to the beverage has been exceptional ever since Sydney's first kegs were filled in 1795. By the end of the 19th Century, when Sydney had 21 breweries, beer-drinking had become popularly associated with manliness; and by the 1930s manufacturers found that advertising which linked their products with sport and physical fitness enhanced sales. The resulting commercial art of the period (right) was also reproduced on glass panels still to be seen in Sydney pubs—gleaming memorabilia celebrating a drink in such demand that more than 70 native brews find a market.

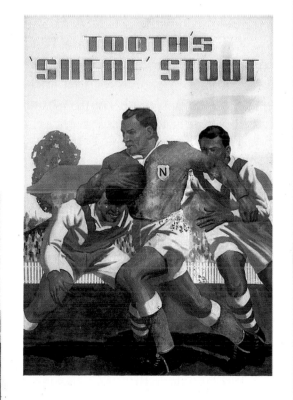

around the beaches in search of the perfect wave, instead of doggedly training in municipal swimming baths. In winter, Sydneysiders devote more leisure hours to watching television programmes—which admittedly include an inordinate amount of sports—than to any other active or inactive pastimes. In Sydney, almost all families possess at least one motor car and a television set. Affluence has led—at least among the younger generation —to a more independent, easy-going society that feels less need for strenuous achievement.

There is, however, one basic attitude towards sport that has barely changed at all: the Australians' deep-rooted passion for winning and for winners. Just as they did a hundred years ago, the mob still stands on "the Hill" at the Sydney Cricket Ground and roars for the imminent destruction of the opposing team. Not long ago, an English friend of mine, standing in their midst, enthusiastically applauded a good drive by an English batsman. A gargantuan pair of hands descended on his shoulders and he looked up to see a giant, who spoke to him very gently: "Something wrong with you, mate? You're supporting the wrong side."

Australians are certainly chauvinistic, but never loyal simply for loyalty's sake. Loyalty, for them, is something that must be deserved, and the allegiance of an Australian supporter can very quickly dissolve if his side turns out to be a bottom-rung team. Such ignominy, it should be stressed, has rarely occurred in cricket, Australia's national summer game. Ever since the first England versus Australia Test Match was played in 1877, Australia has consistently produced cricketers of very high calibre and character. But in 1977, after a century of Test cricket, a curious episode took place in which the national team was disastrously weakened in peculiar circumstances, and the reaction of the cricket-mad public was significant indeed.

Kerry Packer, the Sydney Press and television mogul, made a bid for the television rights to the forthcoming Australia versus England Test series to be played in Australia. His bid was rejected by the Australian Cricket Board, which deemed it unfitting that one television network should have the exclusive rights. Packer, in true Aussie tradition, fought back. He secretly signed up more than 50 of the world's outstanding players, including many of the best Australians and West Indians, and a number of English and Pakistani stars. He then announced that he would stage his own televised international matches. It was an incredible coup, equal to buying all the top baseball players in the U.S.A. and dividing them into teams for one's own "World Series". It was also a move that infuriated and alarmed the cricket establishment in Australia and abroad.

Subsequently, in the 1977-78 season, an Indian team visited Australia to play a Test series against the official national team selected by the Australian Cricket Board from players who had not signed with Packer. At the same time, Packer staged his own "international" series in a bold gamble that his all-star matches would prove the greater attraction. His gamble failed. The majority of fans chose to watch the official matches, in which India and the "second string" Australian team proved to be reasonably well matched. Packer's rebel organization lost several million dollars.

One year later, in the 1978-79 season, it was the turn of England's cricketers to visit Australia for an official Test series. This time it soon became evident that the Australian team, without its Packer-signed stars, was severely outclassed and, consequently, rather than go along to watch Australia lose to England, thousands of fans preferred to watch the gimmicky Packer-style cricket—that included one-day games and floodlit matches—in which their countrymen were playing very successfully. This switch of loyalties caused the Australian Cricket Board to suffer enormous financial losses; and the outcome was that the board had to make a deal with Packer on the terms he had always wanted. He received exclusive rights for the next three years to televise international cricket in Australia, and in return agreed to co-operate with the authorities by disbanding his teams.

It is not only at the top level of sport that Australians display an all-consuming passion for winning. A salutary lesson in their fierce competitiveness may be gained at any inter-school Rugby match on a winter Saturday. The teams fling themselves at each other, urged on by the spectators—usually a posse of fathers running up and down the sidelines and bellowing homicidal instructions to their sons—as if the game were some gladiatorial battle in the Roman Colosseum.

Most Sydney schools teach their pupils Rugby Union football, the rough-and-tumble 15-to-a-side game that, according to tradition, was born in 1823 when William Webb Ellis, a boy at England's Rugby School, broke the rules of soccer by picking up the ball during a match and running with it in his arms. But in Sydney no fewer than four different versions of football are played. Apart from Rugby Union, strictly an amateur sport, there is Rugby League, a 13-to-a-side professional version played predominantly in the Australian states of New South Wales and Queensland, in New Zealand, the north of England and France; soccer, played by both amateurs and professionals, and in Sydney supported mainly by European immigrants; and Australian Rules football, an 18-to-a-side game, peculiar to Australia, that was invented in the mid-19th Century by combining elements of soccer, Rugby and the Gaelic football originally played in Ireland.

Of these, Rugby League is by far Sydney's most popular spectator sport, and it has given birth to a phenomenon of considerable social significance. Before the Second World War, the local League sides developed modest social clubs, providing little more than a bar and perhaps a billiard table and a dartboard for their players and supporters. Since the war, however, many of these clubs have developed into gargantuan multi-purpose leisure centres, which now have an enormous influence on the city's social life.

The Leagues Clubs have long since ceased to be geared solely to the interests of their professional teams. They are veritable entertainment

Slot-machines line the gambling hall in one of Sydney's Rugby Leagues Clubs. Legalized in 1956, the devices contribute millions of dollars annually in taxes.

A Passion for "Pokies"

Social life in the suburbs flourishes around recreational clubs, many of them run by returned servicemen's or sporting organizations. Sydney has more than 500 such clubs and the majority have prospered on the money raked in by their poker-machines. The Sydneysiders' passion for this kind of mechanized gambling is so great that profits from the "pokies" have financed the development of enormous many-sided leisure complexes such as the Eastern Suburbs Leagues Club shown on these pages. Deriving more than half its income from poker-machines, the club is able to provide its 50,000 members with lavish entertainment and recreational facilities for minimal annual dues.

The faces of gamblers—engrossed in spinning the one-armed bandits Australians call "pokies"—assume a mask of concentration with each pull of the lever.

industries in themselves, attracting tens of thousands of members—both men and women—and grossing many millions every year. The St. George League's Club in Kogarah, south Sydney, is an especially impressive example. Founded in 1952, it now occupies huge premises that are nick-named "the Taj Mahal" because of their palatial grandeur. They include four restaurants, numerous bars and cocktail lounges, billiard, television and reading rooms, plus a vast auditorium for staging professional concerts, musicals, plays and variety shows, and for showing films. Its membership, totalling 50,000, embraces people of all ages over 21—and with a variety of interests, since the club encompasses more than a dozen sub-clubs including sections for cricket, indoor bowling, golf, squash, fishing, darts, water-skiing and photography.

An enthusiasm for club life—very much in keeping with the tradition of "mateship" extolled by Australian writers in the 1890s—greatly influences the pattern of leisure in Sydney. The city has clubs catering to every con-ceivable interest—from kite-flying to yoga, from pigeon-racing to growing gladioli. Moreover, in addition to the Leagues Clubs, which thrive in Sydney, there is one other superclub organization of vast wealth and scope: the Returned Servicemen's League, a nationwide association founded after the First World War and subsequently given a new injection of life by the veterans of the Second World War and then of Korea and Vietnam.

Following a visit to Australia in 1922, the British novelist D. H. Lawrence concluded that the R.S.L. was positively fascist in character. It is still essen-tially right-wing in outlook and, with headquarters strategically placed near the centre of Australian political power in Canberra, it represents a powerful pressure group, and concerns itself vociferously with government policies on such things as defence spending and unemployment. But the majority of its more than 250,000 members have only the average working man's interest in politics. They belong primarily for the purpose of enjoying, at very reasonable cost (membership fees are only a few dollars a year), the excellent social and recreational facilities that the R.S.L. provides.

Both the R.S.L. and the Leagues Clubs provide variety and cabaret entertainment on the grandest scale. How do these clubs acquire such wealth when they are essentially non-exclusive with relatively low subscrip-tions and membership fees? Their booming prosperity is firmly founded on one major source of income: the profits taken from their "one-armed bandits", otherwise known as fruit-machines or, as Australians always call them, "pokies" (short for poker-machines). On any night of the week, in one of the big Sydney clubs, you can see the same scene: the jackpot-hunters standing before rows of gleaming machines and, for hour after hour, like automatons, performing the ritual of "feeding the pokie" with the left hand and pulling the lever with the right.

It has been said that if, on a winter's evening, half the population of Sydney is watching television, then the other half is down at the clubs,

At "Les Girls", one of the best known of the many exotic nightclubs that flourish in Sydney's neon-lit King's Cross district, an all-male troupe stages an extravagant transvestite revue.

drinking and playing the pokies. This may be a gross exaggeration; nevertheless it is undeniable that Australians are inveterate gamblers and it is an unusually strong-willed Aussie who, with time to spare, can pass the pokie without pausing for some so-called "bobbertooing" (putting in a bob or two). In Sydney, the pokie-playing urge is so strong that a major club such as the St. George will make a gross yearly income of more than $4 million from its machines—and this despite the fact that they are generously programmed to pay out almost 90 per cent of the money fed into them.

Gambling is a major Australian pastime, and the dominant forms it takes are horse-racing, greyhound-racing and the state-run lotteries. The lotteries involve the greatest number of people (almost every Sydneysider sooner or later buys a ticket); but, in terms of money laid down, horse-racing is the most important form of gambling, accounting for an estimated 75 per cent of all gambling expenditure in Australia (over $2,500 million a year).

Yet gambling does not constitute the biggest casual expense by Sydneysiders in their pursuit of pleasure. That distinction has long been held by the Australians' almost obligatory accompaniment to sporting or social activity: drinking beer, wine or spirits. In the early 1960s, annual per capita consumption of beer was almost 23 gallons. This figure has risen to about 30 gallons, while Australians have increasingly taken to other forms of alcohol too—wine-drinking, for instance, having almost trebled in the last 15 years.

Soon after the founding of the colony, the new Australians became notorious for their excessive drinking—a vice largely arising from the use of rum as a common article of barter and as "incentive payments" to labour. Inevitably, as the tough colony struggled towards respectability, a strong temperance movement emerged, which by 1916 had succeeded in imposing severely restricted licensing hours. But such restraints served only to increase consumption as Australians, faced with 10 a.m.-to-6 p.m. pub hours, determinedly sought to consume the maximum amount of drink within the limited time. More reasonably, the licensing hours for pubs in Sydney have been extended, but opposition to the sale of alcohol on Sundays continues to be strong, especially among church groups. No restrictions, however, have applied to the clubs, whose licensed sale of cut-price drinks to members constitutes an additional factor in their immense popularity and profitability.

The style of public drinking has changed markedly in Sydney during the past few decades. The brick-and-tile utilitarian bars, where men stand shoulder to shoulder swilling vast quantities of beer, are being replaced more and more by well-furnished taverns, where men and women can eat and drink together. At the same time, wine bars—full of ethnic atmosphere and scampi-in-a-basket chic—have sprung up all over the city, resulting in a boom for the New South Wales wine industry, centred in the Hunter Valley, 120 miles to the north.

But this is not to suggest that Sydneysiders have taken to exercising greater moderation. In this city, drinking—like the sea and sun and sex—is regarded by most men, and not a few women, as a fundamental ingredient of the good life. Beer-swilling, with its macho connotations, remains the great masculine pastime—a pleasure to be pursued as though prohibition were just around the corner. And it is still not unusual to find Sydneysiders measuring the success of a party by the degree of drunkenness achieved: good marks for guests "chundering" (vomiting), better marks still if guests become totally paralytic and have to stay the night.

On the popular entertainment level, it is undeniable that no Australian city can rival Sydney in terms of vitality and honest-to-goodness vulgarity. Sydney's Soho-like King's Cross quarter, a small, somewhat sleazy area around Darlinghurst Road and Macleay Street, is full of blaring dance-halls, seedy snack-bars, strip clubs and clip-joints that provide their clients with the company of hostesses.

Yet there is another side to Sydney that totally belies the city's ill-founded reputation as a place populated by Philistines dedicated to mindless physical and sensual pursuits. It now has a most vigorous cultural and intellectual life. There are three universities in the metropolitan area; a fine public library and some fascinating museums, and altogether some 150 art galleries. Until the 1970s the city remained sadly lacking in major theatres and concert halls, but that deficiency has been greatly remedied. Sydney does not have a Broadway or a Shaftesbury Avenue; instead, it can boast the world's most imaginatively designed centre for all the performing arts: the Opera House.

In 1954 a group of city elders proposed that a great arts centre be built on Bennelong Point, the peninsula of land beside Sydney Cove where Captain Arthur Phillip landed to found the new colony. Subsequently, an international design competition, attracting more than 200 entries, was won by Joern Utzon, a young Danish architect. His drawings, envisaging a complex of four halls and theatres roofed by a series of gigantic interlocking shells, were sensationally original. They also contravened most of the rules originally laid down for the competition, including the specification that the main hall should seat up to 3,500 and be suitable for large-scale opera.

Controversy attached to the progress of Utzon's Opera House from the planning in 1957 to the final completion—16 years of political rows, intrigues, union wrangling and delays leading to ever-soaring pre-inflation costs. Estimates for the construction rose from $7.2 million in 1957 to a projection of $85 million in 1968. After innumerable conflicts with government officials, Utzon resigned in 1966 with only the exterior of his creation completed. Critics lambasted the enterprise as a madcap and worthless bid to create the world's largest and most absurdly extravagant "eggshell".

In the end, however, all the years of agonized disputes and appalling expense (ultimately $104 million, provided largely from the profits of a state lottery) were justified when the architectural masterpiece was completed. The Opera House—opened by Queen Elizabeth II in 1973—was hailed as "the building of the century", a work of true genius. Its bold, sweeping curves contrasting dramatically with towering new skyscrapers nearby, the soaring shells of its elliptical roofs ingeniously echoing the shapes of the sails of passing yachts, it brought a new artistic dimension to the harbour's confused and colourful scene. Above all, its white gleam effectively offset the steel-grey bulk of the dominant Harbour Bridge.

Today, facing each other across Sydney Cove at the narrowest part of the harbour, the two structures represent two separate stages in the city's advancing maturity. The bridge reflects both the confidence and pragmatism of Sydney in the 1920s; the Opera House symbolizes the idealism and growing sophistication born in the 1950s. Yet, basically, I feel that their messages are the same. Both are large, chest-thumping gestures that declare: "We can be successful at anything, and we will show the world that we spend our money unstintingly."

The fact that the bridge was an absolute necessity does not diminish the validity of my point. After all, in the 1920s, a more modest suspension bridge would have sufficed instead of a hump-backed colossus visible— and compelling attention—from almost every part of the city. Nor does it matter that both bridge and Opera House were actually designed overseas, owing as much to foreign as to Australian ingenuity. The notion behind them is essentially Australian: to draw the eyes of the world towards a great

Australian city and to proclaim the emergence of a dynamic, self-confident civilization in the Southern Hemisphere.

In social terms, of course, the Opera House may be seen as Sydney's most incongruous construction. It is supremely arrogant in style. It has taken the name of an élitist, somewhat old-fashioned art. Yet it belongs to a modern people who, by and large, eschew all pretentiousness and who pride themselves on their strictly egalitarian principles. The city early developed a happy knack of demolishing class divisions; and in one respect it has demonstrated it once and for all with the Opera House. The story of how this came about is, as they say, "pure Sydney".

From the beginning, it was recognized that the Opera House, being built in the busiest sector of the city, would desperately need its own parking facilities. The original plans provided for a large underground car park to be built beneath the adjoining Royal Botanic Gardens. But then, as the Opera House was nearing completion, conservationists pointed out that the excavations needed to build the proposed parking area would disturb the roots of three very old Moreton Bay fig trees growing on "green land" protected by law from development. Among the objectors was Jack Mundey, boss of the builders' union, who threatened to withhold his members' labour from the project if the authorities attempted to have the protected area derestricted. In the end, the government was compelled to scrap its car park scheme entirely.

The result leaves me with mixed emotions. On the one hand, when attending the Opera House, I may experience considerable frustration in driving around the area again and again, before finding a parking space in the upper reaches of Macquarie Street, three-quarters of a mile away. On the other hand, my democratic sensibilities are warmed by the sight of so many wealthy citizens, dressed in their evening finery, making the trek to the Opera House on foot, or else standing about long after a performance has ended while their chauffeur-driven cars jockey for position outside the main entrance.

I have seen opera in most of the great houses of the world. Never have I felt more at ease than in the unintimidating atmosphere of the Sydney Opera House. Perhaps that is because such a many-sided complex for the performing arts should never have come to be known as an Opera House at all. Opera does not qualify as its prime function, and Sydney has so few passionate opera-lovers that there was only a mild rumble of disapproval in 1967 when—in a move that would have created a public scandal in any major European city—the main, 2,690-seat hall was appropriated by the Sydney-based Australian Broadcasting Commission for its own concerts, with performances by visiting orchestras also to be given there. Opera was then allocated a smaller, 1,547-seat hall, which it now shares with ballet. A third auditorium serves as a theatre, and the complex has a fourth hall intended for general use by classical musicians, pop groups and

New Year's Eve revellers pack the Opera House forecourt for an outdoor concert that launches the annual Festival of Sydney, a month of civic entertainments.

Showcase for the Arts

A geometric fantasy in concrete, the Opera House is Sydney's most spectacular architectural feature. Its roof, covered with more than a million light-reflecting tiles, rises like glittering sails from the harbourside at Bennelong Point. Designed by Danish architect Joern Utzon in 1957, the multi-purpose centre for performing arts took 14 years to build and by the time of its completion had cost $104 million—more than 14 times the original estimate. But the scale of the enterprise has been justified by the public response: every year more than one million people visit the complex to attend performances that are staged daily in its Concert Hall, Opera Theatre and the two smaller auditoriums.

Red-robed choristers simulate a Christmas tree at a seasonal show held in the main Concert Hall.

On stage in the Opera Theatre—the smaller of two main halls—soloists of the Australian Ballet Company dance a pas de deux in Khatchaturian's "Spartacus".

In the Concert Hall, Sydney-born soprano Dame Joan Sutherland—supported by members of the Australian Opera—exults in her role as Léhar's "Merry Widow".

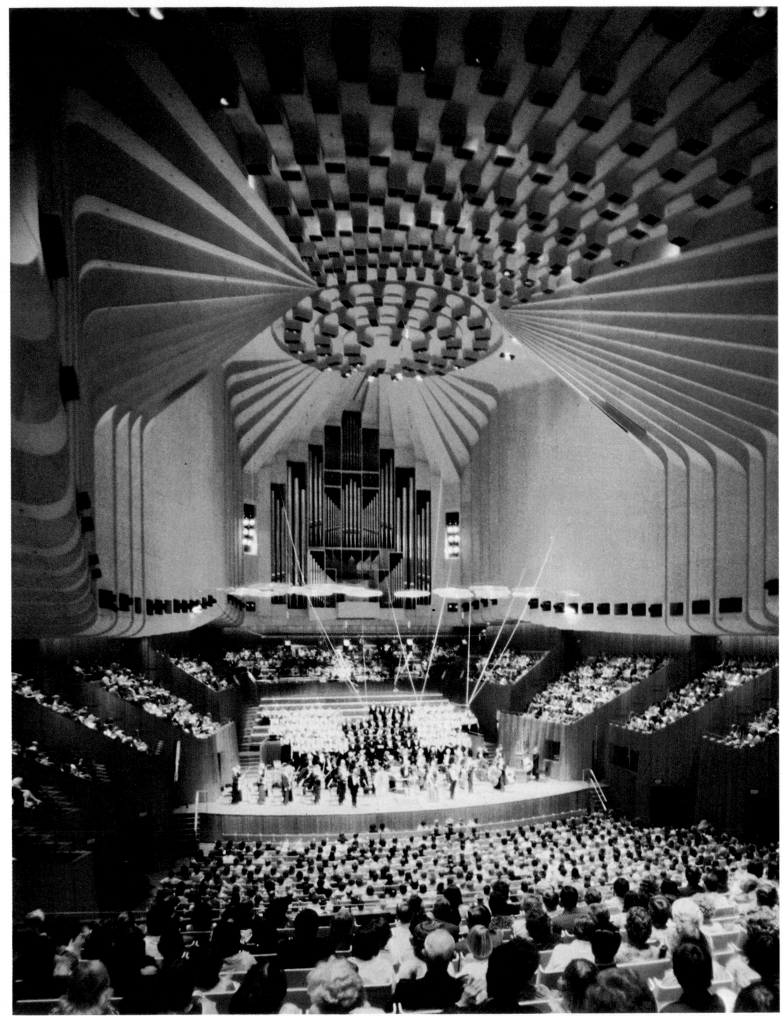

Musicians acknowledge applause beneath an 80-foot fluted birchwood ceiling that contributes to the Concert Hall's superb acoustics as well as to its décor.

individual guest artists. In addition there are facilities for film shows and conferences, together with rehearsal and recording studios.

Nevertheless, I think it absolutely right that the name of such a grandiose project should celebrate the most elaborate and costly of the arts. The interior functions are, basically, irrelevant. Sydney's Opera House—like the Parthenon in Athens, the Escorial Palace near Madrid, or Rome's Vittorio Emanuele Monument—was, in essence, designed to be seen.

On a clear day, looking down on that extraordinary building from the heights of the Harbour Bridge, I find it entirely possible to day-dream about Sydney eventually flourishing as a great capital of the arts as well as of commerce. And that is a dream I could not have contemplated in my wildest flights of imagination when work on the Opera House began, nor indeed in the late 1960s when it was already evident that Sydney would have one of the finest and most imaginative modern buildings in the world.

Back in the 1960s, Australia's culture was still essentially what it had always been: a client of the West. Most of its books, films, television programmes and popular music originated in Britain or the United States. There was no lack of native creative energy and talent, but the public in general was still notoriously suspicious of original creation blossoming in its midst: it still tended to denigrate home-made artistic products or refer to them in patronizing terms.

Some outstanding creative talents soldiered on in Australia when they were more appreciated abroad—among them, most notably, the writer Patrick White, who, for a long time, lived the life of a recluse in the Sydney suburb of Castle Hill, and continued, in short stories and drama, to make scathing attacks on Australian society and to tell his fellow Sydneysiders that they were enemies of excellence, frightened of the solitude of the human soul, and becoming alienated from humanity by isolating themselves from the centres of world civilization. But many of Australia's creative and performing artists—following a long-established pattern—chose to leave the country, some taking up permanent residence overseas, others hoping to establish such a formidable reputation abroad that they could return home as recognized masters of their arts.

The building of the Opera House fairly reflected Australia's keen desire to be noticed in the artistic world. At the same time, however, Australia's sense of cultural inferiority was so great that it had given rise to a form of chauvinistic masochism popularly known as the "cultural cringe", a phrase that magnified a simple belief that the arts were better executed abroad into a paranoid conviction that the artistic world was somehow united in a vast conspiracy directed against Australia.

Fortunately, this gigantic inferiority complex has been disappearing. It began to dissolve in the early 1970s, when Gough Whitlam's reforming Labor government launched a new drive to encourage writers and artists by sponsoring tours, and awarding grants and fellowships—a policy that had its most spectacular success in bringing Australia's film industry to vigorous life. Simultaneously, a new wave of Australian nationalism prompted a renaissance in literature and art. Within a few years the number of art galleries in Sydney multiplied more than tenfold, and suddenly its bookshops were displaying an overwhelming majority of works by Australians on every conceivable aspect of Australian life and history. By 1973, the *Sydney Morning Herald* was sufficiently impressed by the change of mood to comment: "The public will not suffer, tomorrow, the kind of cultural cringe it once felt when confronted by the home-created product." That same year, Patrick White won his Nobel Prize for Literature.

This is not to suggest that Sydney is developing a fast-growing population of aesthetes. In truth, the boisterous attractions of fairgrounds are infinitely more representative of Sydneysiders' tastes than the classical productions in the Opera House. But at least their tastes are their own and, on the cultural level, no longer significantly influenced by a respectful awareness of "parent" cultures. No more is the overseas expert arriving from London or New York automatically accepted as the authoritative guru. The advantages of cheaper jet travel and television by satellite have enabled Australians to escape their age-old sense of isolation. Now, as they can clearly and quickly observe the political and social problems of the world, and of Europe and America in particular, they are much more sceptical about foreign advice and less willing to follow blindly trends and fashions from across the globe.

In the final analysis, I believe the key to any subjective view of a city's attractions is very closely bound up with those aspects one recalls most vividly and readily when long and far away. What is it about Sydney that I remember most? The answer, predictably, is a beach—but not a chaotically crowded and colourful beach like Bondi, nor an intimate beach like Tamarama. In moments of day-dreaming idleness, whenever my thoughts drift back to Sydney, I find myself thinking of a relatively ordinary beach—one like Newport, 16 miles north of the city centre. Newport may not be found in the tourist brochures; but its appeal lies in its very ordinariness and simplicity.

The beach itself is a gentle arc of warm, reddish sand. It has a nondescript utility shed for bathers to change in, a concrete paddling pool for toddlers, a grassy park fronting the sea and, beyond it, a street of quick-food stands, chemists', confectioners' and neighbourhood shops. Along the front grow Norfolk Island pines, though indigenous trees are losing the battle against man-made changes in their environment. The housing is a jumble of ordinary buildings—modest dwellings with sandy backyards and "home-unit" blocks of two or three storeys more suited to the inner suburbs.

There is nothing stylish about Newport. But eight months of the year it is sunny and warm enough for swimming; the surf rolls in majestically, not savagely; the water is of an intense indigo hue, but still miraculously clear. Typically, out to sea, two lines of bathers are visible: the experts, sporting beyond the point where the surf curls just before breaking; the less adventurous idling in the shallows and ducking under the largest waves. The majority of people, however, are on the beach, stretched out on towels or under umbrellas, cat-napping or reading paperbacks. The somniferous summer air is redolent with the tang of sun-tan oil, cigarette smoke and ozone. And all is peaceful, except for the shark-patrol helicopter passing overhead, an over-loud transistor, or some safety warning or announcement—perhaps about a lost child—crackling out from the loudspeakers of the life-saving club. Before the sunbathers there stretches the apparent infinity of the Pacific Ocean; behind them lies the Great Australian Loneliness—the vast, almost empty continent to whose edge the city clings; around them spreads the Great Australian Ugliness of ribbon development and unplanned building.

At last the sun-toasted beachcomber picks up his belongings, calls his children together, gets into the car and heads back into the heart of the immense city that stretches itself sybaritically beside the warm sea. Skyscrapers, high-rise, insurance Gothic, the harbour's branches like so many arms of a water god—it is all manifestly there. So are the Opera House, the bridge, the slowly moving lights of the city's tortuous traffic. And so too is Sydney's airport, stretching its tongue of reclaimed land out into Botany Bay. London is only 24 hours away by jet—but why, asks the Sydney denizen, bother to go there? Australia is no longer cut off and Australians are not bereft of culture or company.

There stands Sydney to prove it—once the lowest and least favoured habitation known to civilized man, a struggling settlement grimly pitted against a hostile country; now observably one of the great cities of the world.

Playgrounds by the Pacific

On Freshwater Beach, just north of Manly, life-saving clubs gather among surfboards and rescue equipment to parade before the judges at a weekend carnival.

More than 30 beaches, sun-drenched and salubrious, line Sydney's Pacific coastline like ribbons of golden sand, broken by rocky headlands. Providing a convenient escape from urban pressures, strands such as Bondi and Tamarama are a mere five miles from the city centre. In summer they are jam-packed —the crowds adding to nature's spectacle, as gregarious sun-worshippers form a colourful mosaic beneath the vault of the sky. "Surf carnivals"—in which rescue teams demonstrate their life-saving skills and compete for medals—can attract as many as 3,000 participants. But at less-frequented beaches, such as Avalon and Whale Beach, an hour's drive from central Sydney, the throng can be avoided; and on the steep promontories flanking even the busiest beaches, contemplative fishermen cluster in small groups to cast their lines into the waves below.

Competing off Bondi Beach, life-savers race around a marker buoy aboard special rescue craft, known as "surf-skis", that combine features of both surf-board ar

anoe. Often preferred to heavier boats because of their speed and manoeuvrability, surf-skis are used as standard equipment by the life-saving clubs for inshore rescues.

Sydneysiders glory in the sun over Tamarama Beach, south of Bondi. Many city workers make the 15-minute drive to the shore to sunbathe during lunch-breaks.

Several beaches permit the uninhibited to uncover their tops to achieve an almost all-over sun-tan.

At Avalon Beach near Sydney's northern limit, bathers use a shark-proof pool built inside a natural rock barrier.

Fishermen lining the rocks near Bondi Beach cast for snapper fish in the surf. Intrepid anglers sometimes use climbing equipment to reach inaccessible cliffs.

Bibliography

Barnard, Marjorie, *A History of Australia.* Angus & Robertson Publishers, Sydney, 1962.
Baume, Michael, *The Sydney Opera House Affair.* Thomas Nelson (Australia) Ltd., Melbourne, 1967.
Blainey, Geoffrey, *The Tyranny of Distance.* Macmillan Company of Australia Pty. Ltd., Melbourne, 1968.
Blainey, Geoffrey, *Triumph of the Nomads.* The Macmillan Press, Ltd., London, 1976.
Boyd, Robin, *The Australian Ugliness.* Penguin Books Ltd., Harmondsworth, Middlesex, 1963.
Cobley, John, *Sydney Cove 1788.* Hodder & Stoughton Ltd., London, 1962.
Cobley, John, *The Crimes of the First Fleet Convicts.* Angus & Robertson Publishers, Sydney, 1970.
Freeland, J. M., *The Australian Pub.* Melbourne University Press, Melbourne, 1966.
Godwin, John, *Australia on $15 a Day.* Arthur Frommer Inc., New York, 1978-79.
Grabosky, Peter N., *Sydney in Ferment.* Australian National University Press, Canberra, 1977.
Gunther, John, *Inside Australia and New Zealand.* Hamish Hamilton, Ltd., London, 1972.

Herman, Morton, *The Architecture of Victorian Sydney.* Angus & Robertson Publishers, Sydney, 1956.
Horne, Donald, *The Lucky Country.* Penguin Books Ltd., Harmondsworth, Middlesex, 1964.
Horne, Donald, *Death of the Lucky Country.* Penguin Books Ltd., Harmondsworth, Middlesex, 1976.
Horne, Donald, *Money Made Us.* Penguin Books Ltd., Harmondsworth, Middlesex, 1976.
Lacour-Gayet, Robert, *A Concise History of Australia.* Penguin Books Ltd., Harmondsworth, Middlesex, 1976.
Larcombe, Frederick A., *The History of Botany 1788-1970.* The Council of the Municipality of Botany, Sydney, 1963.
Learmonth, A. M., *The Australians.* David & Charles, Ltd., Newton Abbot, Devon, 1973.
Millar, T. B., *Australia in Peace and War.* C. Hurst & Co. (Publishers) Ltd., London, 1978.
Moffitt, Ian, *The U-Jack Society.* Ure Smith Pty. Ltd., Sydney, 1972.
Park, Ruth, *The Companion Guide to Sydney.* Collins Sons & Co. Ltd., Sydney and London, 1973.
Philipp, Franz, *Arthur Boyd.* Thames & Hudson Ltd., London, 1967.

Pringle, John D., *Australian Accent.* Chatto & Windus, Ltd., London, 1958.
Southern, Michael (ed.), *Australia in the Seventies—A Survey by the Financial Times.* Penguin Books Ltd., Harmondsworth, Middlesex, 1973.
Spearitt, Peter, *Sydney Since the Twenties.* Hale & Iremonger Pty. Ltd., Sydney, 1978.
Stephenson, P. R., *The History and Description of Sydney Harbour.* Angus & Robertson, Ltd., London, 1967.
Sunset Books, Editors of, *Australia.* Lane Publishing Co., California, 1977.
Tench, Captain Watkin, *Sydney's First Four Years.* Angus & Robertson Publishers in association with Royal Australian Historical Society, Sydney, 1961.
Walker, Kath, *My People.* The Jacaranda Press Pty. Ltd., Milton, Queensland, Australia, 1970.
Whitaker, Donald P., et al., *Area Handbook of Australia.* U.S. Government Printing Office, Washington, D.C., 1974.
White, Patrick, *Voss.* Eyre & Spottiswoode, Ltd., London, 1958.
Younger, R. M., *Australia and the Australians.* Robert Hale & Co. Ltd., London 1970.

Acknowledgements and Picture Credits

The editors wish to thank the following for their valuable assistance: Caroline Alcock, London; Mr. and Mrs. David Ashley-Wilson, Sydney; staff of the Reference Library, Australian High Commission, London; Dr. Jean Battersby, Sydney; Franco Belgiorno-Nettis, Sydney; Peter Bertelle, Sydney; Julie Bolton, London; David Brown, Director of Public Relations, and the staff of the Opera House, Sydney; Richard Carlisle, Great Bookham, Surrey; Paul Dobson, Sydney; Alan T. Duncan, Sydney; Ian Duncan, London; Michael Errington, Sydney; Lady Mary Fairfax, Sydney; Fellowship of First Fleeters, Sydney; Ian Frykberg, London; John Green, Sydney; Peter Jamieson, Teddington, Middlesex; Jonathan King, Melbourne; Kodak Australia Ltd., Sydney; Jeremy Lawrence, London; Glen Lehman, Sydney; Bernard Leser, London; staff of the London Library; Christopher MacLelland, London; David Moore, Sydney; National Parks and Wildlife Service, Sydney; Nature Conservation Council of New South Wales, Sydney; staff of the New South Wales Government Offices, London; Winona O'Connor, London; Bill Rankin, Sydney; Ron Robertson, Sydney; Beverley Ryan, Sydney; Sandra Salmans, London; Dr. Andrew Schachtel, High Wycombe, Buckinghamshire; Michael Schwab, London; Mr. and Mrs. Harry Siedler, Sydney; Adrian Snodgrass, Sydney; Dr. Peter Spearitt, Sydney; Margaret Stoneman, London; Surf Life Saving Association, Sydney; Mr. and Mrs. David Teplitzky, Sydney; Pat Tookey, London; Malcolm Turnbull, Sydney; Pamela Vickery, Sydney; Charles Widdy, Sydney; Dr. Robert Withycombe, Sydney; Giles Wordsworth, London; World Wildlife Fund, London.

Quotation on page 82 from an article by Peregrine Worsthorne in *The Sunday Telegraph* newspaper, March 11, 1979, reproduced by kind permission of *The Sunday Telegraph*, London.

Sources for pictures in this book are shown below. Credits for the pictures from left to right are separated by commas; from top to bottom by dashes.

All photographs are by Brian Brake except: Pages 12, 13—Map by Hunting Surveys Ltd., London (Silhouettes by Norman Bancroft-Hunt, Caterham Hill, Surrey). 38—Permission of the Trustees of the British Museum (Natural History). 40, 41—Thomas Gosse 1765-1844 *Founding of the settlement of Port Jackson at Botany Bay in New South Wales* coloured mezzotint N.K. 11590 in the Rex Nan Kivell Collection in the National Library of Australia, Canberra. 47—Edward Dayes 1763-1804 *Brickfield Hill and village on the High Road to Parramatta* watercolour in the Petherick Collection in the National Library of Australia, Canberra. 55—Mitchell Library, Sydney. 58, 59—National Library of Australia, Canberra. 64, 65—Tyrells Book Shop Pty. Ltd., Sydney (negative Collection). 66, 67—Mitchell Library Sydney. 68, 69—Tyrells Book Shop Pty. Ltd., Sydney, (inset) from the George Lipman Collection. 70—From the George Lipman Collection in the Mitchell Library, Sydney. 71—Mitchell Library, Sydney. 72, 73—Art Gallery of New South Wales Archives, (inset) Mitchell Library, Sydney. 111—Australian Information Service. 121—Australian Centre of Photography, Sydney. 122, 123—National Library of Australia, Canberra. 125—Associated Press. 176, 177—Robert McFarlane Rapport Photos.

Index

Numerals in italics indicate a photograph
or drawing of the subject mentioned.

Filmsetting by C. E. Dawkins (Typesetters) Ltd., London, SE1 1UN.
Printed and bound in Italy by Arnoldo Mondadori, Verona.